LEADING WITH CULTURAL INTELLIGENCE

The Real Secret to Success

SECOND EDITION

David Livermore

Foreword by Soon Ang, PhD
and Linn Van Dyne, PhD

⁄AMACOM

American Management Association

New York • Atlanta • Brussels • Chicago • Mexico City • San Francisco
Shanghai • Tokyo • Toronto • Washington, D.C.

Bulk discounts available. For details visit:
www.amacombooks.org/go/specialsales
Or contact special sales:
Phone: 800-250-5308
Email: specialsls@amanet.org
View all the AMACOM titles at: www.amacombooks.org
American Management Association: www.amanet.org

This publication is designed to provide accurate and authoritative information in regard to the subject matter covered. It is sold with the understanding that the publisher is not engaged in rendering legal, accounting, or other professional service. If legal advice or other expert assistance is required, the services of a competent professional person should be sought.

CQ is a trademark of the Cultural Intelligence Center, LLC.

Library of Congress Cataloging-in-Publication Data

Livermore, David A., 1967-
  Leading with cultural intelligence : the real secret to success / David Livermore ; foreword by Soon Ang, Ph.D., and Linn Van Dyne, Ph.D.—Second edition.
     pages cm
  Includes index.
  ISBN 978-0-8144-4917-2 (hardcover)—ISBN 0-8144-4917-4 (hardcover)—ISBN 978-0-8144-4918-9 (ebook)—ISBN 0-8144-4918-2 (ebook) 1. Leadership—Cross-cultural studies. 2. Organizational behavior—Cross-cultural studies. 3. Management—Cross-cultural studies. 4. Intercultural communication. 5. Cross-cultural orientation. I. Title.
  HD57.7.L589 2015
  658.4'092—dc23
                               2014030865

About AMA
American Management Association (www.amanet.org) is a world leader in talent development, advancing the skills of individuals to drive business success. Our mission is to support the goals of individuals and organizations through a complete range of products and services, including classroom and virtual seminars, webcasts, webinars, podcasts, conferences, corporate and government solutions, business books, and research. AMA's approach to improving performance combines experiential learning—learning through doing—with opportunities for ongoing professional growth at every step of one's career journey.

Printing Number

18 19 20 PC/LSCC 10 9 8 7

For Linda . . . my ultimate soul mate,
fellow sojourner, and love.

CONTENTS

We are pleased to write the foreword to David Livermore's latest book on cultural intelligence (CQ). As academics with a scientific–practitioner ethos, we pioneered the measurement and research of cultural intelligence. Dave then built upon this scientific body of knowledge with his extensive experience researching and working with leaders around the world.

Few people can translate technical academic work into clear and lucid material. Dave has done just that with his books on cultural intelligence, and this one is no exception. He understands the importance of evidence-based management principles and emphasizes research-based scientific evidence rather than anecdotes as the basis for his key points.

Since the first edition of *Leading with Cultural Intelligence*, there has been a large increase in the number of scholars and practitioners using cultural intelligence around the world. Dave has included many of these updated findings and examples in this second edition. This research includes predictors of CQ, outcomes of CQ, and more complex models that include mediation and moderation. *Leading with Cultural Intelligence* presents a view of leadership that is solidly grounded on the latest cultural intelligence theory and research with actionable information for managers and employees.

This book is suitable for people in all sorts of leadership positions. It is especially relevant to global leaders; members of multicultural teams; human resources managers; management training and development professionals; organizational researchers; and students in management, psychology, and other disciplines. It should be valuable to anyone who wants to understand the factors that are critical to effective leadership in our multicultural, global world.

It is indeed a rare privilege to write the foreword to the next edition of a book that has become a quintessential guidebook for culturally intelligent leadership in the twenty-first century and beyond.

—Soon Ang, PhD
Goh Tjoei Kok Chair and Professor in Management
Center for Leadership and Cultural Intelligence
Nanyang Business School
Nanyang Technological University, Singapore

—Linn Van Dyne, PhD
Professor in Management
Michigan State University
East Lansing, Michigan

One time I was speaking to a group of emerging leaders at a symposium in Prague. After a couple of days at the conference, my U.S. colleague based in the Czech Republic said to me, "Okay, Dave. Tell me who you think the strongest leaders are in this group."

Without missing a beat I said, "Oh, that's easy, it's Vaclav and Branka. You can just tell by watching them." "I knew you'd say that," he replied. "And they'd probably be great leaders back in the U.S. But the very thing that would help them succeed as leaders in the U.S.—their charisma, enthusiasm, self-effacing humor, and intuitive style—will be the very things that are stumbling blocks for them here." Then he proceeded to point out to me which individuals in the group he viewed as the strongest leaders for this context. I couldn't believe it. I never would have picked them. But sure enough, a couple of years later, they were the organization's top leaders in the region.

Many leadership and management books give us the idea that leadership is a universal skill set that works the same anywhere. It sounds promising, but it just doesn't jive with the realities of leading in today's multifaceted, globalized world. Yet global leaders don't have the time to master the ins and outs of every cultural difference they encounter. Furthermore, many of the traditional approaches to cultural differences are outdated. For example, can we really say that all Chinese are one way and all Indians are another? I'm not sure we ever could but especially not today. Neither is it sufficient to simply work on being more culturally sensitive. Sensitivity is a start but then what—how do we lead effectively across borders?

This is a book about leading with cultural intelligence. Cultural intelligence, or CQ, is *your capability to function effectively in intercultural contexts*, including different national, ethnic, organizational, generational, and many other contexts.[1] It's also an overall model for thinking about effective, global leadership. It's rooted in academic research of over forty thousand global professionals from more than seventy countries. And it's a form of intelligence that can be developed and learned by anyone. This book will help you develop your cultural intelligence, and as a result, you'll gain a critical edge for leading effectively in today's globally connected world. It's less about mastering all the dos and don'ts of every culture you encounter—something that's close to impossible if you work with as many different cultures as many of us do. And it's more about developing an overall adaptability as a leader to motivate, negotiate, and accomplish results in whatever situation and cultural context you find yourself.

Why This Book?

The purpose of this book is to show you how to lead with cultural intelligence. Rooted in rigorous, academic research, this book reveals the capabilities most consistently found in effective global leaders, and it gives you a four-part model that can be used in any intercultural situation.* Nobody ever leads across cultures perfectly. But by developing these four capabilities, you can improve the way you lead and relate across numerous national, ethnic, and organizational cultures. And for those who have already learned this through the school of hard knocks, the cultural intelligence model offers you a way to share what you've learned with others you lead.

There's an abundance of books and models on global management and cross-cultural leadership. Many of these have informed my own thinking and practice. But even with the growing number

---

* Technically the term *cross-cultural* refers to two cultures interacting, and *intercultural* refers to several cultures interacting; but throughout this book I've followed the norm of using these terms interchangeably simply for ease of writing and reading.

of resources available, 70 percent of international ventures fail because of cultural differences.² Simplistic approaches that teach universal leadership principles are ill suited to today's global landscape. On the other hand, some books on culture and leadership are so complex and cerebral that it's tempting to toss them aside as little more than ivory-tower rhetoric.

Leading with Cultural Intelligence provides a coherent, research-based framework for leading successfully across diverse cultural contexts. It's written for professionals working in a wide range of settings, including business, government, and nonprofit. The four-part model presented in this book can be applied to any multicultural situation.

Second Edition

The first edition of *Leading with Cultural Intelligence* opened doors for me to talk with global leaders all over the world. It's been an incredibly humbling, gratifying experience to hear so many leaders from such varied contexts describe how the research referenced in the book put language and empirical findings around ideas they had been thinking about and working on for a long time. In addition, these conversations challenged me to think about many points that could be added, changed, or improved in the book. Those conversations and constructive comments combined with six more years of research on cultural intelligence and global leadership led to the revised edition of the book.

The core of the second edition is the same as that of the first: reviewing the four capabilities of cultural intelligence and describing their relevance to your leadership. But each chapter has updated material and reflects my own development as a culturally intelligent leader. I'm a different leader today than I was when the first edition came out in 2009. As a result, I found that every page needed some updating with additional examples, new research findings, or stories about some of the great leaders and organizations I've been privileged to encounter since the first edition was released. I suspect I'll have a similar reaction to this version of the book in another six years.

Research Basis

The cultural intelligence model is rooted in rigorous empirical work. Business professors and researchers Chris Earley and Soon Ang built upon the research on multiple intelligences to develop the conceptual model of cultural intelligence.[3] Based on that conceptual framework, Ang collaborated with Linn Van Dyne to create a twenty-item Cultural Intelligence Scale (CQS), which they developed and validated to measure CQ across multiple cultures.[4] The validation process included large samples of students and professionals from various cultures around the world. CQ predicts many important aspects of intercultural effectiveness, most of all, intercultural adjustment and performance. Since 2003, CQ has attracted worldwide attention across diverse disciplines, with studies from academics around the world published in more than a hundred academic journals. Although most thoroughly tested in business and educational contexts, data have also been collected from the fields of health care, engineering, law, social work, science, mental health, government, and religion.[5]

The research referenced throughout the book comes from a number of these researchers, including myself. My initial research looked at how short-term travelers engage cross-culturally—including study-abroad students, charitable volunteers, and itinerant business travelers. My findings revealed a number of gaps in how travelers engaged with the local cultures they encountered; but many of the proposed solutions I reviewed touted the need for travelers to stay home until they learned the language, customs, and norms for whatever culture they wanted to visit. As much as I'd love to master the language and cultural nuances of any culture I visit, it's completely unrealistic. Like many global professionals, I travel widely but not deeply. I just finished a teleconference with people from seven countries and next week I'm heading off on a trip that will include meetings and presentations in five different countries. And that doesn't begin to include the many organizational, generational, ideological, and other subcultures I encounter on any given day. And my experience is not unique. Even those leaders who aren't regularly jumping on a plane are faced with managing people and projects from a variety of cultural backgrounds—particularly when you include different ethnic cultures, regional cultures across the same country, and endless subcultures found in various organizations and communities.

For those of us who travel widely but not deeply, it's simply unrealistic to use the traditional approach to cultural awareness and global management. Nor can we dismiss the reality that culture plays a significant role in how we lead.

I was in the midst of this quandary when I met Soon Ang from Nanyang Business School in Singapore. A mutual colleague introduced us and I made an instant friend. Professor Ang generously shared her research findings with me, and soon thereafter, she introduced me to her colleague Professor Linn Van Dyne at Michigan State University. Many years later, the three of us along with dozens of other researchers are pushing the cultural intelligence research deeper and broader with a relentless commitment to doing research that is rigorous and relevant.

How to Read This Book

Think of *Leading with Cultural Intelligence* as a field guide to understanding and developing cultural intelligence in yourself and others. Cultural intelligence isn't a destination per se but an ability that serves as a compass for guiding us through the globalized world of leadership. Nobody gets to the end of this journey. But with some effort, we'll perform better. Many seasoned leaders have learned how to lead with cultural intelligence through the school of hard knocks. While there's no substitute for hands-on experiences, the cultural intelligence research and model provides a paradigm for a seasoned leader to transfer some of that experience to others.

Chapter 1 explains the relevance of cultural intelligence to global leadership. Although most leaders readily acknowledge the multicultural landscape of today's leadership journey, many still view it as a "nice-to-have" soft skill rather than a non-negotiable. We'll review some of the concrete reasons why an ability to read and adapt to different cultures will make or break you as a leader. Chapter 2 gives a brief introduction to the research on cultural intelligence and directs you to resources where you can learn more. Chapters 3–7 present the most important material in the book: the four capabilities of cultural intelligence and how to apply and develop them as a leader. Chapter 8 describes the return on investment (ROI) from leading with cultural intelligence, and Chapter 9 presents best practices for developing a culturally intelligent team.

Global leadership isn't something I approach solely from the perspective of academic research and theory. I've spent the past couple of decades in leadership roles with people from a vast array of cultural backgrounds across multiple continents. I have as many failures as successes in my own attempts to lead cross-culturally, many of which I'll share along the way. And I've spent the last several years researching the phenomenon of global leadership in others. The book includes research data exemplified through real-life stories to offer best practices for cross-cultural leadership.

What an exciting time to lead! It's virtually free to talk with someone on the other side of the world. The causes dear to our hearts can touch the lives of people living fifteen time zones away.

We get to learn from leaders working and managing in vastly different places from our own. We can eat nachos in Bangkok, sushi in Johannesburg, and baklava in Omaha. We can tap the accounting skills of professionals in Bangalore and Vancouver. And despite rising fuel costs, the opportunity to see the world firsthand and interact with people from around the planet has never been more possible. With cultural intelligence, we can engage in our rapidly shrinking world with an underlying sense of mutual respect and dignity for people everywhere and better accomplish our personal and organizational objectives. This book provides a pathway for gracefully and successfully embarking on the journey into a shrinking world. I look forward to sharing the journey with you.

David Livermore, PhD
Grand Rapids, Michigan

Part I

Cultural Intelligence for Global Leaders

....

CHAPTER 1

CULTURE MATTERS: WHY YOU NEED
CULTURAL INTELLIGENCE

Leadership today is a multicultural challenge. Few of us need to be convinced of that. We're competing in a global marketplace, managing a diverse workforce, and trying to keep up with rapidly shifting trends. But many approaches to this leadership challenge either seem way too simplistic (e.g., "Smile, avoid these three taboos, and you'll be fine") or way too extreme (e.g., "Don't go anywhere until you're a cross-cultural guru"). Cultural intelligence (CQ) offers a better way. The four capabilities presented in this book can help you navigate any intercultural situation.

What are the biggest hindrances to reaching your goals personally and professionally? How do you effectively lead a culturally diverse team? What kinds of cultural situations bring you the greatest level of fatigue? How do you give instructions for an assignment to a Norwegian team member versus one from China? What kind of training should you design for an implementation team coming from multiple cultural backgrounds? How do you get feedback from a colleague who comes from a culture that values saving face above direct, straightforward feedback? And how can you possibly keep up with all the different cultural scenarios that surface in our rapidly globalizing world? These are the kinds of questions that will be answered by developing your cultural intelligence.

All my life I've been fascinated by cultures. From as far back as when I was a Canadian American kid growing up in New York, I was intrigued by the differences my family would encounter on our trips across the border to visit our relatives in Canada. The multicolored money, the different ways of saying things, and the varied cuisine we found after passing through customs drew me in. I've learned far more about leadership, global issues, and my faith from cross-cultural experiences and work than from any graduate course I've ever taken or taught. I've made people laugh when I've stumbled through a different language or inadvertently eaten something the "wrong" way. I've winced upon later discovering I offended a group of ethnically different colleagues because I spent *too* much time complimenting them. I'm a better leader, teacher, father, friend, and citizen because of the intercultural friendships I've forged through my work. And through the fascinating domain of cultural intelligence, I've discovered an enriched way to understand and prepare for my work across borders.

Cultural intelligence is *the capability to function effectively across national, ethnic, and organizational cultures.*[1] It can be learned by most anyone. Cultural intelligence offers leaders an overall repertoire and perspective that can be applied to myriad cultural situations. It's an approach that includes four different capabilities, enabling us to meet the fast-paced demands of leadership in the global age. This book describes how to gain the competitive edge and finesse that comes from using these four capabilities to lead with cultural intelligence. Think about a cross-cultural project or situation facing you. Take a minute and walk through the four capabilities of CQ right now:

1. CQ Drive: What's your motivation for engaging with the cultural dimensions of this project?

2. CQ Knowledge: What cultural differences will most influence this project?

3. CQ Strategy: How will you plan in light of the cultural differences?

4. CQ Action: How do you need to adapt your behavior to function effectively on this project?

If you don't have a clue how to answer some of these questions, I'll get to all that. But before more fully describing cultural intelligence and how to develop it, we need to spend a few minutes understanding its relevance to leadership.

From West Michigan to West Africa

It's the day before I fly to Monrovia, the capital of Liberia. Liberia, a small country on the coast of West Africa, isn't a place I ever planned to visit. But given that the university where I was working had formed a partnership there, it became a regular destination for me. I've spent far more time working in Europe, Asia, and Latin America, much more familiar destinations to me than West Africa, which still feels very foreign. Yet the flattened world of globalization makes even the most foreign places seem oddly familiar in some strange way. Wireless access in the hotel where I stay, Diet Coke, and the use of U.S. dollars remove some of the faraway feeling of a place like Monrovia. Even so, I still have to make a lot of adaptations to do my job in a place like Liberia.

It's amazing how life and work in our rapidly globalizing world brings us an unprecedented number of encounters with people, places, and issues from around the world. I guess the world is flat—isn't it? Journalist Thomas Friedman popularized the term *flat world* to suggest that the competitive playing fields between industrialized and emerging markets are leveling.[2]

The day before I leave for West Africa is spent tying up loose ends prior to my weeklong absence. I respond to emails from colleagues in Dubai, Shanghai, Frankfurt, and Johannesburg and I talk on the phone with clients in Kuala Lumpur and Hong Kong. My wife and I grab a quick lunch at our favorite Indian restaurant, and we talk with the Sudanese refugee who bags the groceries we pick up on the way home. Before my kids return from their Cinco de Mayo celebration at school, I call my credit card company and I reach a customer service representative in Delhi. Even in the small city of Grand Rapids, Michigan, where I live, intercultural encounters abound.

One would think travel across the flattened world would be easier than it is. Getting from Grand Rapids to Monrovia takes some very deliberate planning and it wreaks havoc on the body. The travel and work have to be planned around the three days a week when Brussels Air, the only Western airline that flies into Monrovia, goes there. But still, the fact that I can have breakfast with my family one morning and go for a run along the Atlantic Coast in West Africa less than twenty-four hours later is pretty amazing. So maybe the world is becoming flat.

On the flight from Brussels to Monrovia, I sit next to Tim, a twenty-two-year-old Liberian guy currently living in Atlanta. We chat briefly. He describes his enthusiasm about going "home" to Liberia for his first visit since his parents helped plan his escape to the States during the civil war ten years ago.

As we land, I see the U.N. planes parked across the tarmac. Eight hours earlier I was walking the streets of Brussels and grabbing an early morning waffle. And now I am making my way toward passport control in Monrovia. Maybe travel across multiple time zones isn't so bad after all.

Eventually I end up at baggage claim next to Tim, my new acquaintance. A porter who looks so old he could pass for a hundred is there to help Tim with his luggage. The porter asks Tim, "How long are you staying here, man?" Tim responds, "Only two weeks. I wish it was longer." The porter bursts out with a piercing laugh. "Why, my man? You're from America!" Tim responds, "I know, but life is hard there. I wish I could stay here longer. Life is better here." The porter laughs even harder, slaps Tim on the back, and says,

"You're talking crazy, man. Look at you. You have an American passport! You don't know what a hard life is. I've been working the last thirty-seven hours straight and they haven't paid me for six weeks. But I can't give up this job. Most people don't have jobs. But look at you. You've been eating well. You look so fat and healthy. And you live in the USA!" Tim just shakes his head and says, "You don't know. You have no idea, no idea. It's hard. Never mind. Just get my bag." I see the fatigue penetrating Tim's broad shoulders.

I can understand why the porter found it absolutely laughable that a twenty-two-year-old bloke who can afford a two-week vacation across the ocean could consider life "hard," yet I imagine there are some significant hardships for Tim as a young Liberian guy living in Atlanta. The statistics are stacked against him. How many people lock their car doors when he walks by? What extra hoops did he have to go through to get hired at the fitness center where he works? And Tim told me the enormous expectations put upon him by his family and friends who stayed in Liberia. After all, they didn't get to escape the war, so the least he can do is send regular amounts of money to support them. Observing these kinds of interactions as we travel provides insights into how to negotiate and fulfill our strategic outcomes.

As I walk out of the Monrovia airport, a brightly smiling woman adorned in glowing orange from head to toe sells me a SIM card for my phone for USD $5. I hand her 5 *U.S.* dollars. I send a text message to my family to let them know I arrived safely. While walking, texting, and looking for my driver, I nearly trip over a woman relieving herself, I see kids selling drinking water, and I pass men my age who by Liberian standards are statistically in their final years. Using my smartphone to send a text message home makes the foreign seem familiar. But watching my kids' peers sell water makes the same place seem foreign.

After a decent night of sleep, I go for a morning run along the muddy streets by my hotel. I keep passing children carrying buckets of water on their heads from the nearby well. Breakfast at the hotel where I stay occurs at a large dining room table where guests are served two runny eggs, a hot dog, one piece of plain white bread, and a cup of instant coffee. On this particular morning, the breakfast table includes U.N. consultants from India and Sweden, an economist from the United States, some North American business professionals, and a British physician.

I begin talking with the U.S. businesswoman seated next to me. She works for a U.S. company that sells baby food. She tells me this is her fifth trip to Monrovia in the last two years. After her first trip, she convinced her company there was a growing market for baby food in Liberia, particularly among the many Liberians who were coming back after living abroad during the fifteen-year war. While overseas, these Liberians had seen the nutritional benefits and convenience of baby food and they were sure they could convince their fellow Liberians to buy it as well. The company shipped several containers of baby food. They selected the kinds of food to send based upon market research of the Liberian diet; but the company used the same packaging used in the United States: a label with a picture of a baby on it. The company launched its product with many promotions including free samples for parents to try with their kids, but very few people picked up the samples, and even fewer purchased the baby food, despite it being introduced at a very low price. Sales of the baby food flopped until the company suddenly realized that African grocery distributors usually place pictures of the *contents* on their labels. Therefore, marketing a jar with a baby on the front didn't sell. Oops!

Hearing the businesswoman's story, the white-haired British doctor sitting across from us chimes in with a story of his own. He tells us how he shipped several crates of medicine from London six months ago but it still hasn't arrived in Liberia. He had called and emailed the Monrovian shipyard from London every couple of days for the last few months and was continually told the shipment hadn't arrived yet. Once he reached Monrovia, he went to the dock almost daily to inquire whether his shipment had arrived. Each time he was told, "Come back tomorrow. It will definitely be on the next ship." But it never was. He is beginning to think he'll never see the medical supplies, and the value of his brief sojourn in Liberia is becoming seriously undermined by not having them. He muses that it now seems a waste of time for him to have come.

I go on to share a couple of my own cultural mishaps and we talk about how easy it is to laugh at these things in retrospect, but at the time, the frustration and financial cost involved is anything but a laughing matter. Our breakfast conversation is a reminder of the many challenges that come with leading cross-culturally. And in a few minutes, I am about to discover that reality again myself.

One of the key objectives for my trip to Liberia is to decide whether we should include a Liberian school, Madison College (pseudonym), in the multi-tiered partnership we were developing throughout the country. Our primary organizational contact in Liberia is Moses, a catalytic Liberian who is leading an effort to rebuild the Liberian educational system after the war. Moses is the eldest of his father's eighty-five children and the son of his father's first wife. That makes him the highest-ranking member of his family now that his father is dead. Moses is short and stocky, and he carries himself like a tribal chief. He consistently cautioned our team against working with Madison College. He was concerned about the integrity and ethics of the president of Madison, Dr. Jones. This morning, Moses and I are visiting another key leader in Monrovia, Dr. Harris. Dr. Harris has done a lot of work with Dr. Jones and Madison College. Dr. Harris is a tall, stately looking man who remains behind his desk while we talk, sitting rigid and straight in a navy blue suit.

Drawing upon my value for direct communication, soon after we get through the perfunctory introductions, Dr. Harris mentions that he sometimes teaches at Madison. I take that as my cue. Notice our dialogue:

Dave: How do you like teaching at Madison, Dr. Harris? Is it a good school?

Dr. Harris: Oh, it's a great joy for me to teach there. The students are so eager to learn. . . .

Dave: And how about Dr. Jones? What's he like as a leader?

Notice that while being direct, I am trying to ask open-ended questions, an approach that usually works well for me at home.

Dr. Harris: Madison is a very good school. Dr. Jones has been there for a long time, since before the war.

I can see my open-ended questions aren't getting me very far. My time with Dr. Harris is limited. I need his honest assessment of Dr. Jones, so I decide to go for it:

Dave: I'm sorry if what I'm about to ask is a bit uncomfortable, Dr. Harris. But I've heard some concerns about Dr. Jones and his leadership. I'm not looking for unnecessary details. But we're considering a partnership with Dr. Jones and Madison College. This partnership would result in a high level of investment from our university. Might you be able to offer me any perspective on these criticisms I keep hearing?

Dr. Harris: It would be very good for the students if you partner with Madison College. Our schools have nothing here. The war destroyed everything. It would be very, very good. Please come.

I'm not entirely clueless. I can see what is going on, but I don't have time for what feels like game playing to me. I come at it again.

Dave: Yes, that's why I'm here. But I wonder what you can tell me about Dr. Jones specifically. Would you feel good about endorsing him to us as a significant partner?

Dr. Harris: It's really quite amazing the school survived the war. I mean, of course they had to shut down for a while. The rebel soldiers overtook all of Monrovia. But they were one of the first places to reopen. They have very good people there.

Dave: And you feel good about the way Dr. Jones is leading there?

Dr. Harris: Dr. Jones has done many good things. We've been friends for many years. Actually, we were classmates together in primary school. It would be very good for you to help Madison. I can introduce him to you if you like.

As we walk away from the meeting, I turn quickly to Moses to assure him: "Moses, I don't want you to think I don't trust the validity of your concerns about Dr. Jones. It was just important for me to try to get his input. But that doesn't mean I'm discounting your reservations."

Fortunately, Moses has learned to talk to a bottom-line North American like me in a way that I get it. He replies:

> Don't you get it, Dave?! Don't you see?! Of course he wasn't going to tell you his concerns about Dr. Jones. You should never have asked him that, especially not with me there. He would never speak disparagingly about him in front of another Liberian brother to a complete stranger from the States. They grew up together! What did you expect him to say?

I shoot back:

> The truth! That's what. He doesn't need to give me gory details. But if he is aware of these improprieties Dr. Jones keeps being accused of, I expect him to at least encourage me to explore my

concerns further. If someone asked me about a childhood friend I knew was embezzling money, I'd tell the truth!

Moses explains that Dr. Harris might have delved into this with me a bit if we had been alone. He says, "But it would be shameful to him and me both if Dr. Harris had criticized his childhood friend in front of me to you! And he's teaching there. Talking about this would bring shame to him. You never should have asked him that—not with me there! Never!"

I wasn't totally blind to the cultural and interpersonal dynamics involved here. But I was at an impasse in getting some key information I needed to move forward. Usually I can make my way through these kinds of conflicts when interacting with individuals from cultural contexts similar to mine. But the interpersonal skills and persuasive strategies I use intuitively at home weren't working for me here. This is where cultural intelligence comes in. It helps us effectively adapt our leadership strategies when working with individuals from different cultural backgrounds while still accomplishing what we need to get done. Later, I'll come back to this story to show you how cultural intelligence eventually helped me resolve this dilemma.

Culture and Leadership

Perhaps the world is not so flat after all, especially when you consider that Liberia is closer to the norm for many places in the world than the exception. Like Liberia, most of the world is collectivist, hierarchical, and values saving face above being direct—all ideas we'll address more fully in Chapter 5. More of us move in and out of these stark cultural contrasts almost as frequently as we move from one web page to another. The ease with which we encounter so many cultural differences in a twenty-four-hour period can lead us to underestimate the chasm of difference between one

CULTURE MATTERS FOR LEADERS

Ninety percent of leading executives from sixty-eight countries identified cross-cultural leadership as the top management challenge for the next century.[3] Most contemporary leaders encounter dozens of different cultures daily. It's impossible to master all the norms and values of each culture, but effective leadership does require some adaptation in approach and strategy. The most pressing issues executives identify for why cultural intelligence is needed are:

- Diverse markets
- Multicultural workforce
- Attract and retain top talent
- Profitability and cost savings

culture and the next—whether it's Grand Rapids and Monrovia, France and Germany, or Starbucks and Shell. Friedman's idea of a flattening world is very appropriate when applied to the growing competition and opportunities in emerging economies. But we ought to resist applying the notion of a "flat world" to suggesting we can do "business as usual" wherever we go.

In fact, 90 percent of leading executives from sixty-eight countries identified cross-cultural leadership as the top management challenge for the next century.[4] It used to be that worldwide travel and cross-cultural interactions were largely reserved for state leaders and high-level executives from massive multinational corporations such as IBM and Mitsubishi. Today, most every leader engages in myriad multicultural interactions. For some, that means traveling through passport control to the fascinating worlds of new foods and languages. For others, culturally diverse encounters are as close as their email in-box, the person on the other side of the cubicle, or the 6 a.m. conference call with a globally dispersed team.

An intuitive sense of leadership and expertise in one's field continue to be valuable leadership assets, but they're no longer adequate to truly leverage the global potential that exists. Hospital administrators are overseeing health care professionals who are treating patients from numerous cultural backgrounds. Military officers are giving orders to eighteen-year-olds that if not carried out well will show up as international incidents on BBC and CNN. And business executives are facing growing pressure to recruit and lead talent who can effectively sell and produce services and products that appeal to customers in emerging markets.

Executives report that leading *without* cultural intelligence results in increased time to get the job done, heightened travel time and costs, growing frustration and confusion, poor job performance, decreased revenues, poor working relationships at home and abroad, and lost opportunities.[5] But leading *with* cultural intelligence opens up a number of promising opportunities, including the following:

Diverse Markets

The days of identifying a single target customer are long gone for most organizations. Most organizations and leaders are serving customers whose tastes, behaviors, and assumptions are not only different but often in conflict with one another. Putting a picture of pureed carrots on the front of baby food might reduce sales in a U.S. market, but doing so in Liberia suddenly made the same product more marketable. Describing yourself as a "tried-and-true Midwest company" or a "three-generation, Chinese-owned business" might gain trust with one customer and scare off the next one.

The proportion of revenue coming from overseas markets is expected to jump by an average of 30 to 50 percent over the next three to five years.[6] Coca-Cola sells more of its product in Japan than it sells in the United States. By 2003, 56 percent of U.S.

franchise operators were in markets outside the United States, and for companies like Dunkin' Donuts and KFC, their international presence is far more lucrative.[7] The demand from emerging markets is seen as the most critical factor facing global businesses. The spending power of China and India is increasing at an enormous rate. The *Economist's* *CEO Briefing* reported, "The number of households earning more than USD $5,000 annually will more than double over the next five years in China, and will triple in India."[8] More than 1 billion people are expected to join the emerging middle class over the next ten years.

In 2012, the Economist Intelligence Unit surveyed CEOs from hundreds of multinational corporations around the world. It found that for the first time during an economic recession the majority of CEOs surveyed were planning to expand internationally, rather than retreat, because they believed their greatest opportunities for growth were outside their domestic borders.[9] Seventy percent of Facebook's users are outside North America and its executives expect that percentage to continue to grow. In the last decade, 20 percent of GE's growth came from emerging markets, and it expects that growth to reach 60 percent in the next decade. Amway, headquartered in the small city where I live, derives 90 percent of its revenues from international markets. So even though thousands of Amway's workforce never leave Michigan on the company's tab, they're interacting with colleagues, customers, and issues across the world on a daily basis. The number of Chinese companies expanding globally has reached unprecedented levels and all indicators are that growth will continue. Lenovo, the Chinese personal computer giant, is acquiring companies all over the globe—from Brazil's CCE to Germany's Medion, and a joint venture with Japan's NEC. South African companies have a long history of worldwide mining enterprises, but the last decade has seen a surge in other South African industries expanding across borders, including telecoms, retailers, and breweries such as MTN, Woolworths, and SABMiller, respectively.

Leaders from China, South Africa, Germany, the United States, Japan, and dozens of other countries recognize that some of their greatest opportunities lie in new cultural markets. There's really no such thing as a uniform global culture to which we market. Today's organization and its leaders must be both local and global, or "glocal," in understanding and serving customers.

Multicultural Workforce

The task of managing a diversified and dispersed workforce at home and internationally is another major demand facing today's global leaders. Fostering good communication and building trust have always been two seminal issues in leadership, but learning how to do so among a culturally diverse team is a whole new challenge. Human resources policies, motivational strategies, and performance reviews need to be adapted for various cultural groups represented among your team. In addition, tapping into a global workforce often means outsourcing service to India and manufacturing to China, or it just as well might mean an Indian company outsourcing to the Philippines. Knowing how to measure the costs, benefits, and appropriate expectations involved with these kinds of opportunities is fraught with complexity.

The Global Leadership and Organizational Behavior Effectiveness (GLOBE) study is the most comprehensive global leadership study done to date. The GLOBE researchers examined leaders and followers across sixty-two countries to determine the leadership differences and universals across these diverse cultures. They found that "clarity" is a universal characteristic that followers everywhere want from their leaders. And "unethical behavior" is something followers do *not* want from their leaders, regardless of the follower's culture. But how one defines "clarity" and "unethical behavior" varies widely from one place to the next. Some leaders believe it's more unethical to embezzle funds and other leaders believe it's more unethical to disparage a friend to a foreigner. The longest list of findings from the GLOBE study was the stark *differences* in what followers from one culture want from their leaders versus what followers from another culture want. For example, a participative leadership style in which managers involve others in decision making was viewed as an essential way of working among the German leaders and organizations surveyed. However, this same style was viewed as a weakness among the firms and leaders surveyed in Saudi Arabia. The Saudis believed authoritative leadership demonstrated clarity and strength.[10]

Many of these cultural preferences for leadership style are related to the values embraced by a culture as a whole. We'll look at these more fully throughout the book. But the challenge of leading in today's multicultural world is that you often have team members from diverse places such as Germany and Saudi Arabia on the same team. These differences leave many teams stalled in gridlock. However, when managed with cultural intelligence, a multicultural team offers organizations several benefits. It offers built-in expertise for diverse markets, it provides an around-the-clock workforce, and when managed well, it offers some of the greatest potential for innovation. In fact, few things have more potential for promoting innovative ideas than diverse perspectives. But it's not automatic. One study examined the influence of diversity on the extent to which team members would speak up. When CQ levels were low, homogeneous teams outperformed diverse teams in how much they would speak up and develop innovative ideas. However, when CQ levels were high, diverse teams significantly outperformed homogeneous teams in generating innovative ideas. The high-performing, diverse teams had developed a coherent strategy for aligning expectations, minimizing conflict, and maximizing the diverse perspectives, which resulted in better solutions.[11]

You might not be able meet the preferences and demands of every personality and cultural difference represented on your team. But cultural intelligence will help you make better use of the differences on your team to build trust, reach targets, and accomplish results. We'll look at how to do this, including developing some shared standards that transcend differences, while also seeing how cultural intelligence allows you to adjust and adapt your leadership style depending on the colleague or team member.

Attract and Retain Top Talent

Cultural intelligence is also needed by global leaders to address the challenge of recruiting, developing, and retaining top talent. Up-and-coming leaders in emerging economies have many options at their disposal, and they're seeking firms and executives who demonstrate culturally intelligent practice. Katherine Tsang, CEO of Standard Chartered Bank China, responded to this challenge by creating what she called a superhighway for attracting and retaining young, globally minded leaders. Her mantra to her team is "Go Places!" It's a double entendre for working with a global network of affiliates and growing a personal portfolio in global leadership. Tsang identifies the race for good talent as one of the most pressing reasons her company must become more culturally astute.[12]

Cultural intelligence is particularly important for those individuals sent on international assignments. Of all managers given overseas assignments as expatriates, 16 to 40 percent end them early. Cultural issues are the cause of 99 percent of these early terminations, not lack of job skills. The cost of each failed expatriate assignment has been estimated anywhere from USD $250,000 to more than USD $1.25 million when expenses associated with moving, downtime, and myriad other direct and indirect costs are included.[13]

Cultural intelligence is also becoming a growing necessity for employees who never take an extended overseas assignment. More and more employees are expected to take short trips overseas to work with colleagues and customers or to work with international clients from home. Organizations practicing cultural intelligence are more likely to recruit and retain the talent needed to meet these demands.[14]

Profitability and Cost Savings

Bruce Brown, chief technology officer at Procter & Gamble, talks about the costly lesson the company learned in the 1990s when it was trying to push global products that could be sold everywhere, while others were paying more attention to what local consumers wanted in various markets. Unicharm, a local Japanese competitor of P&G's, was introducing novel products that were doing much better than P&G's global ones. Brown says, "It was a harsh lesson around the importance of delighting consumers. The consumer is the boss, not the global program or the manufacturing equipment. I learned that you can be common around the world but you also need to be unique enough to delight local consumers."[15]

In contrast, A. G. Laffey, CEO of P&G, insists on getting to know the tastes and interests of local consumers. In fact, Laffey says he will only travel somewhere in the P&G world if two things are arranged for him: an in-home visit with a consumer and a store-check. His recent visit to Istanbul involved sitting with a Turkish woman in her house and watching her wash dishes and clothes. He talked to her for ninety minutes and then walked the aisles of a local store. He wanted to see how P&G products were shelved as well as competitive products. The in-home visit is the most important part to him. His insistence on seeing local markets up close stems from his desire to improve his understanding of consumer needs and to send a message to all his executives: If the CEO of an $80 billion company has time to spend a couple hours in a home in Istanbul, maybe you do too.[16]

Culturally intelligent leadership increases profits, reduces costs, and improves efficiencies when marketing and selling products in new markets. An expat with cultural intelligence will get up to speed on the new assignment much more quickly, which in turn makes better use of the costly expense of sending talent overseas. The tie to profitability shows up in other ways as well. For example, rarely a week goes by without a report in the news about how some company or public figure has blown it by making a culturally insensitive comment that shines a poor light on the reputation of the organization and its products and services. But leaders who handle these kinds of issues appropriately build trust and build the value of their organizations.

Competitive advantage, increased profits, and global expansion are central to why many of us are interested in cultural intelligence; however, most of us would readily agree we're also interested in behaving in a more respectful, humanizing manner with the people we meet throughout our work. Cultural intelligence can help us become more benevolent in how we view those who see the world differently from us. The *desire* and *intent* to treat other people with honor and respect don't automatically mean our *behavior* comes across as dignifying and kind. Most people and cultures agree that some measure of civility is appropriate, but definitions of civility are culturally bound. Various adaptations are necessary in order to ensure that others feel we are treating them with respect, honor, and dignity. This kind of adaptability requires cultural intelligence. An ability to effectively relate and work across cultures is an essential part of survival. And with cultural intelligence, global leaders not only survive but also thrive in the twenty-first-century world.

Global Leadership Myths

Culture matters. It's more than just a "nice-to-have." It's a key factor in what makes or breaks today's global leader. As a result, organizations in every sector are clamoring to find effective global leaders. Those who can lead with cultural intelligence are in demand. Yet much of what gets talked about in the global leadership space is informed by myths and anecdotes rather than empirical evidence. Even many top-rated MBA programs assure prospective students and employers that their curriculum will develop global leadership, yet there's little done to measure and develop global capabilities in their students. And most organizations rely most on technical expertise when looking at whom to put in charge of a new, global project. I regularly encounter the following myths when reading, listening, and talking with others about global leadership:

Myth #1: Leadership Is a Sixth Sense

Conventional wisdom among many business executives is that leadership is a sixth sense: You either get it or you don't. You have to lead from the gut. And frankly, there's some research that backs up the surprising strength of seasoned executives using their gut more than data or detailed analysis to make good decisions. That's because the "gut" has been subconsciously programmed through years of experience. The problem is, the subconscious programming is specific to a culture and may not be a reliable source when making split judgments and decisions in an unfamiliar culture. This explains why some individuals have been incredibly successful leading in one context only to fail miserably when attempting to lead in another. The "sixth sense" of leadership has to be retrained and developed when the cultural context changes.

Myth #2: The World Is Flat

I've already acknowledged my appreciation for Friedman's compelling argument that the economic playing field has been leveled globally.[17] A Filipino start-up firm can go head-to-head with a behemoth multinational company, and leaders in all contexts are wise to wake up to this reality. But I often hear people applying

Friedman's idea more broadly than it was intended. I'm regularly asked, "Isn't there a global professional culture emerging where people are more alike today than different?"

When you observe people in airport lounges in Dubai, Sydney, and London, it certainly seems like we're all more alike than different. And if you predominantly experience different cultures by visiting hotels and offices that are built for guests like you, it's easy to miss the differences that exist. But when you get beneath the surface, you find we're remarkably different. Leaders have their head in the sand if they think they can lead people the same way everywhere. Culture doesn't explain everything. But it is one of the driving factors in how to effectively negotiate, build trust, foster innovation, and motivate people toward a shared objective.

Myth #3: If No One Follows, You Aren't Leading

Surely a "leader" with no followers might not be leading. *Or* he or she might be attempting to lead in the wrong context. Leadership is not only about the values and style of the leader. As evidenced by the findings in the GLOBE study referenced earlier, not all followers want the same thing from their leaders. The cultural values and preferences of the followers strongly influence who can effectively lead them. Some followers want larger-than-life, charismatic leaders like Bill Clinton. Others want modest, understated, practical leaders like Angela Merkel. This is explained by an idea known as implicit leadership theory, which says that whether you lead effectively is not only based on your leadership skills; it's also a reflection of your followers' expectations of leaders. Because culture is one of the variables that shapes what people expect and want from a leader, a culturally intelligent leader is wise to understand this before accepting a new leadership role or assigning someone else to one.[18]

Myth #4: Matrix Models Are Better Suited for Leading Across Borders

Many companies have moved away from headquarter-centric models of leadership to matrix models. Reporting lines go in multiple directions, teams are co-located, and decision making is more collaborative than top-down. Most of the world, however, prefers a more hierarchical style of leadership in which authority lines are explicit and followers are given clear, specific directions. There's great potential in matrix models for international growth and expansion. But a matrix model requires an additional level of cultural intelligence in order to effectively use it.

I've interacted with leaders at Google about this. Google has an extremely strong corporate culture and recruiters are given a clear standard of how to spot the Google DNA when searching for new Googlers. But the questions and techniques recruiters typically use to get a sense of a job candidate's interests, personal accomplishments, and innovative ideas need to be significantly adapted based on the cultural background of the candidate. And the ability to find the right candidates who fit with the more matrixed structure of Google requires culturally intelligent recruiters.

Global leadership itself is not a myth. It *is* possible to lead effectively across multiple cultures. This is the very thing we've been studying in our research on cultural intelligence for the last couple of decades. We have growing evidence that a leader's cultural intelligence predicts several important leadership outcomes—something we'll review more explicitly in Part III of the book. Effectively leading across various cultures is a capability that can be measured and improved. But it begins with a more thoughtful, situational understanding of leadership.

Conclusion

I'm sitting in an airport right now. For a split second, I forgot where I was. And the familiarity of the scene around me did little to help. The Body Shop is right in front of me, Burberry is to my left, Starbucks is to my right, and the duty-free shopping store is just around the corner. The guy next to me is typing away furiously on his smartphone. It's easy to see the familiar airport totem poles in Sydney, Sao Paulo, London, Hong Kong, Orlando, and Johannesburg and believe the world is flat in every way. In part, it is. You can order your grande, triple-shot, nonfat, vanilla, no-foam Starbucks latte in sixty-two countries. And endless competitors offer their own versions of the same drink in many more places. But beware of thinking that the same negotiating skills, sense of humor, and motivational techniques can be used indiscriminately with everyone, everywhere.

Leading in the twenty-first-century world means maneuvering the twists and turns of a multidimensional world. The continually shifting landscape of global leadership can be disorienting; experience and intuition alone are not enough. But cultural intelligence offers a way through the maze that's not only effective but also invigorating and fulfilling. Join a community of leaders across the world who are acquiring cultural intelligence to tap into the opportunities and results of leading across our rapidly globalizing world.

CHAPTER 2

WHAT IS CULTURAL INTELLIGENCE?

The vice chairman of one of the largest Fortune 100 companies in the world was speaking to a group of Asian executives in Singapore. The North American chair spent half his keynote telling the audience how much he *loved* Asia. He said, "I spend 200-plus days a year here. . . . I love the food. I just can't get enough of this place. Asia is the future! I come here as often as possible."

The mostly Asian audience seemed to appreciate his enthusiasm for their part of the world. But during the question-and-answer period that followed, things began to unravel for him. One individual asked, "So what are you changing about your business strategy given your commitment to Asia?" The executive looked a little caught off guard and gave a nondescript answer about working on some focus groups to determine that. And then someone else asked who on the company's board is from Asia, to which he said, "Well, we meet quarterly in the U.S. so it's not realistic to fly them to the States that often." And when he was asked what challenges he faces leading people in Asia, he again had nothing of substance to say.

This North American executive was a very articulate speaker. He had a likable personality, an impressive leadership portfolio, and he exuded charisma. But his enthusiasm and charm didn't work with this Asian audience. And when the questions started coming, he was blindsided.

If two candidates for an executive position have similar resumes, will they be equally effective working across borders? Not necessarily. This is one of the unique contributions from the cultural intelligence research. Cultural intelligence isn't something that comes automatically based on where someone has worked, studied, or lived. It's an *individual capability*. Some have it, some don't; but anyone can become more culturally intelligent.

What leads to higher levels of cultural intelligence? Is someone who grew up in London or Singapore more likely to have high CQ than someone who grew up in Des Moines or rural China? Do Millennials have higher CQ than boomers? And what role does international experience and formal education play in your CQ? All these variables can be related to CQ but they're correlations, not causations.[1] I've met business leaders and government officials who have lived for decades overseas yet demonstrate very little ability to see beyond their cultural blinders. And I've met other leaders, sometimes with minimal international experience, who are extremely adept at moving in and out of various cultural contexts and situations while still remaining true to who they are. What makes the difference? *What abilities and skills consistently yield results in effective cross-cultural leadership?*

Who Are the Culturally Intelligent?

The question that has informed our research for the last couple of decades across more than seventy countries is this: *What's the difference between individuals and organizations that succeed in today's multicultural, globalized world and those that fail?* Our desire was to go beyond the existing notions of cultural sensitivity and awareness to identify the recurring characteristics of individuals who can successfully and respectfully accomplish their objectives, whatever the cultural context. Awareness is the first step, but it's not enough. A culturally intelligent leader can effectively manage people and projects whatever the cultural context.

The research, which to date includes survey responses from more than 40,000 individuals across every major region of the world, reveals four capabilities consistently found among the cul-

Figure 2-1. The Four Capabilities of Culturally Intelligent Leaders

turally intelligent, which are depicted in Figure 2-1. These were conceptualized based on the existing research on intelligence, including academic intelligence (IQ), emotional intelligence (EQ), and other forms of intelligence such as social intelligence and practical intelligence. CQ picks up where these other forms of intelligence leave off. It gives you the practical and interpersonal skills needed when the cultural context changes. Each of the four capabilities of cultural intelligence includes more specific skills (subdimensions) that can be measured and enhanced. We'll examine these thoroughly in the chapters that follow but here's a brief overview:

1. *CQ Drive (Motivation): Having the Interest, Confidence, and Drive to Adapt Cross-Culturally.*

   CQ Drive, the motivational dimension of CQ, is your level of interest, drive, and energy to adapt cross-culturally. Do you have the confidence and drive to work through the challenges and conflict that inevitably accompany cross-cultural work? The ability to be personally engaged and persevere through intercultural challenges is one of the most novel and important aspects of cultural intelligence. We cannot simply *assume* people have the interest and motivation to adjust to cultural differences. Employees often approach diversity training apathetically or do it just because it's required. Personnel headed to international assignments are often more concerned about moving and adjusting their families overseas than they are about developing cultural understanding. Without ample motivation for engaging interculturally, there's little point in spending time and money on intercultural training.

CQ Drive includes three subdimensions that can be assessed and developed: intrinsic interest, the degree to which you derive enjoyment from culturally diverse situations; extrinsic interest, the tangible benefits you gain from culturally diverse experiences; and self-efficacy, the confidence that you will be effective in a cross-cultural encounter.[2] All three of these motivational dynamics play a role in how you approach intercultural situations.[3]

2. *CQ Knowledge (Cognition): Understanding Intercultural Norms and Differences.*

CQ Knowledge, the cognitive dimension of the CQ research, refers to your knowledge about culture and its role in shaping how business is done. Do you understand the way culture shapes how people think and behave? It also includes your overall knowledge of how cultures vary from one another.

CQ Knowledge includes two subdimensions that can be further assessed and learned: cultural-general understanding and context-specific understanding.[4] Cultural general refers to a macro understanding of cultural systems and the cultural norms and values associated with different societies. To lead effectively, you need to understand ways that communication styles, predominant religious beliefs, and role expectations for men and women differ across cultures. In addition, general knowledge about different types of economic, business, legal, and political systems that exist throughout the world is important. For example, every nation has cultural systems for how its members distribute products and services or for how they mate and raise their children. Understanding how a family system works might seem unnecessary but it becomes critically relevant when you're trying to develop human resources policies for employees who are expected to care for senior members of their extended family. And you need a core understanding of culture, language patterns, and nonverbal behaviors. This kind of knowledge helps build your confidence when working in a new cultural environment. The value a culture places on time and relationships becomes highly germane when a Scandinavian is trying to get a signed contract from a potential affiliate in China or Saudi Arabia, where different norms shape leaders' expectations.

The other important part of CQ Knowledge is knowing how culture influences your effectiveness in specific domains. For example, being an effective global leader in business is different from being an effective leader of a multicultural university. And working across borders for an information technology company requires a different application of cultural understanding than working across borders for a charitable organization or on a military initiative. This kind of specialized, domain-specific cultural knowledge combined with a macro understanding of cultural issues is a crucial part of leading with cultural intelligence.

CQ Knowledge is the dimension most often emphasized in many approaches to managing across cultures. A large and growing training and consulting industry focuses on teaching leaders this kind of cultural knowledge. Although the information coming from CQ Knowledge is valuable, unless it is combined with the other three capabilities of CQ, its relevance to the real demands of leadership is questionable and potentially even detrimental.

3. *CQ Strategy (Metacognition): Making Sense of Culturally Diverse Experiences and Planning Accordingly.*
CQ Strategy, also known as metacognitive CQ, is your ability to strategize when crossing cultures. Can you slow down

long enough to carefully observe what's going on inside your mind and the minds of others? It's the ability to draw on your cultural understanding to solve culturally complex problems. CQ Strategy helps a leader use cultural knowledge to plan an appropriate strategy, accurately interpret what's going on, and check to see if expectations are accurate or need revision.

The three subdimensions of CQ Strategy, which can be measured and developed, are planning, awareness, and checking.[5] Planning means taking time to prepare for a cross-cultural encounter—anticipating how to approach the people, topic, and situation. Awareness means being in tune with what's going on in ourselves and others during an intercultural encounter. Checking means comparing our actual experience with what we expected to happen. CQ Strategy emphasizes taking the time to plan consciously, and it's the lynchpin between understanding cultural issues and actually being able to use our understanding to be more effective.

4. *CQ Action (Behavioral): Changing Verbal and Nonverbal Actions Appropriately When Interacting Cross-Culturally.*

CQ Action, the behavioral dimension of CQ, is your ability to *act* appropriately in a range of cross-cultural situations. Can you effectively accomplish your performance goals in different cultural situations? One of the most important aspects of CQ Action is knowing when to adapt to another culture and when *not* to do so. A person with high CQ learns which actions will and will not enhance effectiveness and acts on that understanding. Thus, CQ Action involves flexible actions tailored to specific cultural contexts.

The subdimensions of CQ Action are speech acts, the specific words and phrases we use when we communicate specific types of messages; verbal actions; and nonverbal actions.[6] It is these three kinds of behaviors that most need to be adapted to cultural norms. Although the demands of today's intercultural settings make it impossible to master all the dos and don'ts of various cultures, there are certain behaviors that should be modified when we interact with different cultures. For example, Westerners need to learn the importance of carefully studying business cards presented by those from most Asian contexts. And Asians need to engage in small talk to build trust with North Americans. Also, some basic verbal and nonverbal behaviors enhance the extent to which others perceive us as effective leaders. As an example, the verbal tone (e.g., loud versus soft) in which words are spoken can convey different meanings across cultures. And perhaps far more important is the capability to adapt the way you work to different decision-making processes, deadlines, and team dynamics. Almost every approach to intercultural work has insisted on the importance of flexibility. With CQ Action, we now have an evidence-based way of assessing and improving flexibility.

Most of this book is devoted to unpacking these four capabilities and offering you insights for how to strengthen them in yourself and others you lead. As you develop each of these capabilities, you'll tap into all kinds of opportunities in yourself and others.

How Is CQ Measured?

After conceptualizing and testing the four capabilities of CQ, my colleagues Linn Van Dyne and Soon Ang developed the Cultural Intelligence Scale (CQS) and worked on confirming the validity of the CQS using culturally diverse samples that included executives, expats, military leaders, staff, students, and sales agents. The CQS measures a leader's development in each of the four capabilities as well as the subdimensions associated with each one.

The empirical evidence for using the CQS as a valid measurement of intercultural capabilities was first published in 2007.[7] Since then, CQ research has been peer reviewed in over a hundred academic journals. In addition, Van Dyne, Ang, and Koh validated an observer-rated version of the CQS and demonstrated its reliability as a valid way to assess leaders' intercultural capabilities based on feedback from others (e.g., peers, reports, supervisors).[8] The CQS continues to be available to academics for research purposes in order to continue supporting and driving the ongoing research of cultural intelligence by scholars around the world.

CQ is a more reliable, consistent way to predict how you will lead across cultures than your personality, age, gender, where you're from, or emotional intelligence. David Matsumoto, a world-renowned cross-cultural psychologist, identified CQ as one of the only reliable ways to measure cross-border skills. He states, "There is considerable evidence for the concurrent and predictive ecological validity of CQ with samples from multiple cultures."[9] Matsumoto goes on to report that CQ predicts a leader's cross-cultural performance in several areas: judgment and decision making, problem solving, ability to adjust, well-being, ability to sell across cultures, culture shock, innovation, team performance, negotiation, and trust building.[10]

The CQS was used to develop the *CQ Self-Assessment* and the *CQ Multi-Rater Assessment* (360°), both of which are being used widely by leaders in business, government, charitable settings, and universities. The *CQ Self-Assessment* gives leaders a personal inventory of how they perceive their cross-border leadership skills. The *CQ Multi-Rater Assessment* combines one's self-assessment with feedback from others. This assessment provides a more complete and reliable picture of CQ because it allows leaders to compare their self-ratings with how others rate their CQ. Several Fortune 500 companies, government agencies, charitable organizations, and universities are using the *CQ Multi-Rater Assessment* in their leadership development initiatives. (Learn more about CQ assessments and research at www.culturalQ.com.)

Cultural Intelligence vs. Cultural Competence

It's certainly not a novel idea to suggest that leaders need to develop skills to work effectively across cultures at home and overseas. This often is referred to as cultural competence or more recently in some circles as one's "global mindset." How does cultural intelligence relate to these similar concepts? *Cultural competence* is an umbrella term to refer to one's ability to understand, appreciate, and interact with people from different cultural backgrounds. There are more than thirty cultural competence models, which include over three hundred concepts ranging from personal characteristics (e.g., extravert versus introvert) to attitudes and beliefs. Many of these models have contributed significantly to my own understanding of global leadership, but as much as I enjoyed the readings and presentations I heard on many cultural competency theories, I often experienced a disconnect with knowing how to apply them as a leader. The cultural competency field has lacked a coherent model, and many of the corresponding inventories overemphasize awareness, attitudes, and understanding cultural norms. It's nearly impossible to assess and improve these kinds of elusive ideas, and it's demotivating if you learn that your personality predisposes you to be ineffective cross-culturally. And as important as it is to be aware of cultural norms, I've met plenty of people who know a great deal about cultural norms but can't for the life of them lead effectively across different cultures.

Cultural intelligence, while drawing from many of the valuable insights provided from the cultural competence field, differs in the following key areas.

Form of Intelligence

CQ draws on the rich history of the intelligence research.[11] It's included in the *Cambridge Handbook of Intelligence,* along with other research-based forms of intelligence such as emotional intelligence and social intelligence. Emotional intelligence is the ability

33

to detect and regulate the emotions of one's self and others.[12] Most leaders know the critical importance of this capability for leading effectively. But how does emotional intelligence translate into leading across cultures?

I once interviewed a group of MBA students who traveled to Bangalore, India, on a study-abroad program. One of the students, Shelly, was very vocal throughout our time together. She came to the meeting wearing heels, and a black suit, with her hair pulled up in a knot. She offered warm, nonverbal affirmation whenever her peers spoke. It only took a few minutes of interacting with Shelly to see she would probably score pretty high on an EQ assessment. She was an excellent conversationalist, and several times during the focus group meeting, Shelly not only responded to my questions but also found ways to draw in those students who had previously been sitting disengaged. Yet, ironically, when I asked Shelly, "So what was the biggest challenge you faced when you were in Bangalore?" she replied, "Just getting people to talk with me. It was totally awkward. I tried everything I could think of and most of my conversations went nowhere. Even though we speak the same language, we never seemed to get into meaningful conversations."

Individuals who have a strong ability to empathize and relate to people in their own culture might find that the same empathetic and social skills don't always work when interacting with people from a different cultural background. This can be extremely frustrating to someone like Shelly who usually finds social interaction natural. Books and training on emotional intelligence presume a level of familiarity with the culture of those with whom we interact and lead. Cultural intelligence picks up where emotional and practical intelligence leaves off. It allows you to develop and apply your interpersonal and problem-solving skills when working in culturally diverse situations. And because it's a learned form of intelligence, it's something you can apply to any culturally diverse situation rather than thinking you have to relearn how to lead for every new situation or hire.

Coherent Framework

Another way cultural intelligence differs from many cultural competency theories is the coherent framework on which the model is based. The four capabilities of CQ provide a coherent way to measure, enhance, and apply CQ. This is much more practically useful than a long list of competencies that mix together personality traits, attitudes, and learned capabilities. The four capabilities of intelligence (motivation, cognition, metacognition, and behavior) are interrelated, whatever the form of intelligence. A person who knows (cognition) how to relate interpersonally but has no desire to do so (motivation) won't function in a socially intelligent way. An individual who can deeply analyze (metacognition) a practical situation but can't actually solve it in real life (behavior) doesn't have much practical intelligence.

In addition, the coherent model behind cultural intelligence offers a culture-general approach, a need identified in a variety of studies of global management.[13] As mentioned previously, it was this broader approach of cultural intelligence that initially drew me to the research and model. Much of my own work has required regular bouts of short-term, episodic travel. I was convinced culture was a significant force in how I did my work, but I felt paralyzed by the unrealistic notion of becoming a cultural expert on all the different people and places I encountered.

There is certainly a place for learning the specifics of certain cultures. When it became clear I was going to be responsible for leading my university's work in Liberia, I knew I needed to enhance my understanding of Liberia's historical and cultural background. It would have been careless for me to solely rely on a general understanding of cultures to do my work effectively. But I also wasn't starting from zero. Even though I had never been to Liberia, nor had I spent any time studying the culture, a growing measure of cultural intelligence helped me know what kinds of information to seek and the kinds of questions to ask. I've already demonstrated that my previous experiences and understanding didn't keep me from making mistakes. And I have plenty more like those to share. But, thankfully, learning from our mistakes can be one of the greatest ways to improve our cultural intelligence. In fact, part of being more culturally intelligent is embracing the idea that cross-cultural conflict is inevitable and provides an opportunity for personal and professional growth.

You too will need to gain more specific understanding of certain organizational, generational, and socio-ethnic cultures. But the primary emphasis of the cultural intelligence approach is to develop a skill set that can be applied to all kinds of cultural situations. Although some initial reading and training in cultural intelligence can jump-start your growth in cultural intelligence, you will continue to add to your repertoire for culturally intelligent leadership throughout your career. The four-part model behind CQ offers leaders a coherent way to develop cultural intelligence in themselves and those they lead.

Predicts Performance

Understanding one's "intellectual capital" or a leader's level of "ethnocentrism"—dimensions measured on some other intercultural assessments—can be interesting insights. But there's little reliable evidence that these measures by themselves predict a leader's intercultural performance. The four capabilities of cultural intelligence can be mapped to specific outcomes, and there are hundreds of peer-reviewed studies to back this up. If you want to excel at intercultural negotiation, CQ predicts how well you'll do so and sheds light on how to improve. For someone expected to lead a multicultural team, CQ predicts where the leader will have the greatest challenges. Or if you want insights on an individual's decision-making abilities cross-culturally, CQ predicts that as well. The CQ research was designed to predict performance and adjustment in intercultural situations and, therefore, it's best used for that purpose. The specific performance results related to high CQ are reviewed in Chapter 8.

Developmental Approach

People inevitably ask me, Is cultural intelligence *nature* or *nurture?* Are some people just genetically inclined toward being more culturally intelligent? The answer is quite possibly yes. Just as some of us are more naturally oriented to be better runners, engineers, and musicians, so also may some of us be more genetically inclined to be more flexible in our behavior cross-culturally.

For example, the research finds that the capabilities of cultural intelligence that correlate to being an extravert differ from those that correlate to being an introvert. There's also a positive relationship between being naturally conscientious and CQ Strategy. The personality trait referred to as "openness," a general curiosity toward circumstances and the world, is positively related to all four capabilities of cultural intelligence.[14] So there are some interesting correlations between our personalities and cultural intelligence, something we'll explore more fully in Chapter 8. However, the emphasis of cultural intelligence is that *through learning and interventions everyone can become more culturally intelligent.* Just because someone might bear a natural talent in adjusting his or her behavior for cross-cultural situations is no guarantee that the person will be a culturally intelligent leader. In the same way that possessing good genes for long-distance running doesn't mean someone who never exercises can expect to be a marathon runner, so also someone naturally disposed toward openness has to develop that trait in order to lead with cultural intelligence. As one of the contemporary forms of intelligence, cultural intelligence is more focused on nurture than nature. Through training, experience, and accountability, anyone can improve his or her CQ. This is another important distinction of cultural intelligence as compared to some other approaches to global leadership.

Cultural intelligence is uniquely suited to the demands of global leaders. It offers leaders a realistic, practical skill set to meet the demands of leadership in today's fast-paced world. (For ongoing updates about CQ research and materials, visit www.culturalQ.com.)

Four–Step Process

There are a variety of ways to apply the four capabilities of cultural intelligence to leadership. They can be used to assess individuals you're considering for a cross-cultural assignment. They can also serve as four categories for diversity and inclusion programs, global management training, or for a leader's personal development plan. And each of the capabilities can be used as a four-step process for developing cultural intelligence both over the long haul and in case-by-case situations. This four-step process is one of the ways cultural intelligence is applied in this book. Although the four capabilities of cultural intelligence don't always develop in one particular order, it can be helpful to think about the four capabilities of CQ as four steps toward increased CQ.[15] It might look something like this:

- Step 1: CQ Drive (motivational dimension) gives us the energy and self-confidence to pursue the needed understanding and planning necessary for a particular cross-cultural project.
- Step 2: CQ Knowledge (cognitive dimension) provides us with an understanding of basic cultural issues that are relevant to this project.
- Step 3: CQ Strategy (metacognitive dimension) allows us to draw on our cultural understanding so we can plan and interpret what's going on in this situation.
- Step 4: CQ Action (behavioral dimension) provides us with the ability to engage in effective, flexible leadership for this task.

As the process repeats itself, your cultural intelligence has the potential to keep growing. Cultural intelligence is not a static ability. It continues to morph and develop as we go about our daily work. And it doesn't always develop in a linear direction, moving from one step to the next. But if you're looking for a practical way to begin applying CQ to a leadership situation, using the four capabilities as four steps is one way to get started.

An Inside-Out Approach

There's little hope we can adapt our intercultural behavior in any kind of sustained way unless we actually change the way we see our fellow citizens around the world. We have to move beyond artificial approaches in which we *pretend* to be respectful and move toward becoming leaders who *genuinely respect* and value people from different cultural backgrounds. This is a significant factor determining whether a leader truly behaves with cultural intelligence. Diversity programs and creative cross-cultural simulations are pointless if we don't actually change the way we view each other.

One of the complaints I often hear from some employees as they assess diversity training is that it made little difference in what actually occurred in the workplace. It may indeed be helpful to remind men about appropriate ways to interact with their female colleagues, and there is benefit to teaching people different cultural values related to direct versus indirect communication. But if a guy doesn't view his female colleagues with respect or if an Aussie leader still sees her Chinese affiliate as needing to "get to the point," have we really accomplished much?

One study reviewed a company that had developed an extensive diversity training program to address the abysmal morale throughout the organization. Thousands of dollars and many diversity training workshops later, little had changed. Only through a more in-depth analysis did it surface that the CEO of the organization, a former U.S. Marine, was extremely prejudiced against overweight employees. In his view, an overweight worker was an undisciplined, lazy worker. He and his peers had been through numerous modules and interventions for enhancing respect of women and people of color. But the core issue wasn't being addressed.[16] It was an unconscious bias that shaped the whole environment of the company. Leading with cultural intelligence begins with looking internally at biases and assumptions and then making conscious decisions to address them.

Becoming culturally intelligent means we have to do more than simply change the way we talk to our culturally diverse colleagues. We have to actually transform the way we see each other. I'll say more about this transformative approach as we move ahead on our journey toward leading with cultural intelligence.

Conclusion

Some individuals have high CQ and others don't, but almost everyone can become more culturally intelligent. Cultural intelligence is uniquely suited for the barrage of cultural situations facing today's leaders. It includes a set of capabilities needed by leaders in every field. Without it, leaders run the risk of driving their careers and their organizations into obsolescence. But leaders who commit to improving the ways they think, plan, and act through intercultural situations have an unusual edge for navigating the fascinating terrain of our curvy, multidimensional world.

Cultural intelligence is a learned capability that builds on the other forms of intelligence needed by today's leaders. Just as leaders can grow in their social, emotional, and technical competence, they can grow in their ability to effectively lead across various ethnic and organizational cultures. As leaders move through the four capabilities of cultural intelligence—CQ Drive, Knowledge, Strategy, and Action—they gain a repertoire of perspectives, skills, and behaviors that they can use as they move in and out of the fast-paced world of globalization. True cultural intelligence stems from within and transforms the way we lead at home and across the globe.

Part II

Developing Cultural Intelligence

CHAPTER 3

CQ DRIVE: DISCOVER THE POTENTIAL

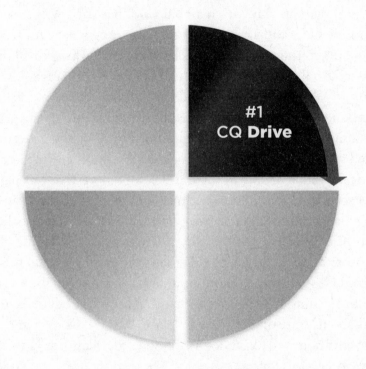

CQ DRIVE: What's my motivation?	
Showing interest, confidence, and drive *to adapt cross-culturally*	
Profile of a leader with high CQ Drive	Leaders with high CQ Drive are motivated to learn and adapt to new and diverse cultural settings. Their confidence in their adaptive abilities will influence the way they perform in multicultural situations.

I'm very energized by cross-cultural encounters. Put me in a room full of people and the internationals in the room draw me like a magnet. Ask me where I want to eat and I'll choose something ethnically exotic. Book me on an international flight and my adrenaline starts pumping. I love to blaze the streets of a new place, savor the local food, roam the neighborhoods, and shop at the local markets. My international work has been well served by my insatiable wanderlust. But sometimes it gets me into trouble. Not all my colleagues and friends have shared my love for all things cross-cultural. One time I was at a conference in Bangkok with a group of Western colleagues and I told them I knew a great little place where we could grab some local tribal food. My suggestion was almost unanimously vetoed, and, much to my chagrin, we ended up at Tony Roma's for steak and ribs. Another time I enthusiastically told a couple of my travel companions that our partner in Mexico had decided to move our upcoming meeting to an outlying village rather than Mexico City. Neither of them was happy about the decision, one replying, "You've got to be kidding" and the other asking, "Why waste all that time getting out there when we could just meet at the comfortable hotel where we always stay?"

I'm learning not to assume that everyone will be as excited as I am about venturing into a new place. We all have varying levels of motivation and drive for working across cultures, and that's okay. Some of us love to travel and experience different places and people. Others prefer never to leave home. But no leader can escape working in a global context today.

Even without an innate passion for all things diverse, there are some simple ways to grow your motivation for leading across cultures. CQ Drive, the motivational dimension of cultural intelligence, is one of the most important findings that emerged from our research on culturally intelligent leaders. Leaders who are effective cross-culturally are curious about and interested in different cultures.

The importance of motivation to intercultural effectiveness may seem painfully obvious. Yet it's an element that is often overlooked. Many organizations jump into training about cultural differences without first assessing whether personnel have any motivation to learn this information and whether they see it as relevant to their performance. This is one of the reasons diversity-training programs often fail. If team members don't see the positive benefits of changing the way they interact with culturally diverse colleagues, the training can be a waste of time. There is a direct correlation between your level of motivation for adapting cross-culturally and your effectiveness. It's not the only component, but it's critical.

Sometimes our reluctance to work with another culture stems from something in our past experience. Take Wendy, for example, a no-nonsense, thirty-seven-year-old professional who grew up in an upper-middle-class home in upstate New York. She went to Cornell, got her MBA at Harvard, and spent seven years climbing the corporate ladder in New York City. She exudes a confidence not easily missed by her straight posture, warm but self-assured smile, and articulate speech. But throughout her studies and work, she had always been a Big Sister to kids in underprivileged neighborhoods. Five years ago, Wendy made a drastic career shift and accepted a job as CEO of a nonprofit organization focused on helping children at risk.

Throughout its fifteen-year history, Wendy's organization has been focused primarily on serving children in under-resourced communities throughout the United States and Canada. Last year, the board charged Wendy with expanding its work into Central America. Wendy didn't support this idea because she was afraid the organization would lose focus, but she agreed to look into it. When I met Wendy, she had spent the past six months reading everything she could about the issues facing children in places such as Tegucigalpa, Managua, and San Salvador. She read about the cultural issues throughout the region and she was even shoring up her Spanish. When Wendy agreed to meet me as part of my research on culturally intelligent leadership in nonprofits, she was two weeks away from making her first trip to Central America on behalf of the organization.

Wendy said:

> Put me with a group of leaders on the south side of Chicago or among a bunch of community activists in rural Saskatchewan and I know what to do. I have a clear sense of how we can serve the needs of children there. But even after all the learning I've been doing about Central America, I still don't have a strong grasp how we should adapt our programs to meet the needs of kids down there.

Frankly, I was encouraged to learn that Wendy wasn't overly confident about how the organization's programs would work there, but I observed an overall reticence in how Wendy talked about this expansion into Central America.

Eventually I asked Wendy, "So are you looking forward to this trip?" She replied, "Ah . . . you know what it's like. Travel gets old fast. But it will be fine. My only visits down there have been a couple of beach vacations in Costa Rica." I continued, "But how about this whole new emphasis into Central America? Are you excited about that added dimension to your work?" She said:

> I can't say I'm excited. I'm trying to learn what I can and then I need to hand off this endeavor to someone with the passion to go at this wholeheartedly. My passion is for kids *here.* It's not that I don't care about kids in other places. But my heart can only take on so much.

After some further interaction, Wendy told me she has a hard time working with Hispanic men. In a previous job, she was repeatedly harassed by a Mexican American colleague, though she never filed a formal complaint against him. She knew it was unfair to generalize her experience to all Hispanic men, but she couldn't change the raw emotions she felt about thrusting herself into an environment filled with men who remind her of this past experience.

Despite Wendy's hard work to improve her Spanish and understanding of Central American culture, her reticence for this cross-cultural project will impede her effectiveness. Many approaches to global leadership focus on information about how cultures differ. But some of the greatest challenges in managing across cultures have much less to do with inadequate information and more to do with internal motivation. Without adequate drive and confidence, leaders will continue to struggle in cross-cultural work. This is one of the first things to look for when assessing the CQ of someone who will be taking on a role that requires leading across cultures. Low CQ Drive should signal caution about whether the individual is ready for this kind of responsibility.

The good news is that any leader *can* increase his or her CQ Drive. Van Dyne and Ang identified three sources of motivation, which can be described as the three subdimensions of CQ Drive: intrinsic interest, extrinsic interest, and self-efficacy.[1] These subdimensions are the basis of the following strategies for improving CQ Drive in yourself and others.

HOW TO DEVELOP CQ DRIVE

1. Be honest with yourself.
2. Examine your confidence level.
3. Eat and socialize.
4. Count the perks.
5. Work for something bigger.

Key question: What's my level of confidence and motivation for this cross-cultural assignment? If it's lacking, what can I do to increase it?

Be Honest with Yourself

The first step for improving CQ Drive is being honest with ourselves. Wendy was able to honestly acknowledge her reservations about immersing herself in the Latin American culture, and that's a significant breakthrough.

Even though I come to life when I'm immersed in a new place, I regularly have my own moments when I hit the wall. They don't have to be all-out meltdowns, and they usually aren't. Take, for example, this journal entry I wrote when facilitating a leadership session with a group of executives in Malaysia:

> I'm jet-lagged, Emily [my daughter] is sick at home, and the session didn't go great yesterday; then after a late dinner with John, I came back to the hotel room to face an in-box full of urgent emails. I need some space to come up with a different approach for the seminar today; but there's no time for that now. I have to jump on a conference call and then I start teaching in an hour.

For me, the lack of motivation stemmed from wanting to be home with my sick daughter, feeling exhausted, and questioning my effectiveness. For Wendy, the lack of motivation was rooted in fear based on a previous experience.

Klaus, a German expatriate on a two-year assignment in Nairobi, Kenya, needed a similar kind of honesty. He described the fear his family experienced when they moved to Nairobi from Munich:

> We found ourselves distrusting everyone. We heard so many stories about expat families being robbed and taken advantage of. My wife resisted hiring domestic help for the longest time for fear of having Kenyans in our home. Eventually we became more relaxed. But the fear factor was a huge challenge for us during our first six months.

Surely it's appropriate to tend to the safety of our families and to find out if we're subjecting ourselves to danger. But then we have to discover ways to overcome our fears and persevere, as Klaus did.

Honesty also requires facing the prejudices and biases we implicitly associate with certain groups of people. Notice the frank, raw musings written by Sharise, a business leader in Portland, Oregon:

> Am I a racist? Yesterday when I stopped to get my blood drawn, a black man walked in. I just assumed he was the lab tech. Only later did it become evident he's a physician. . . . Why did I so quickly assume he must be the lab tech? If he had been a white guy, I probably would have guessed he was a doctor.

We all have unconscious biases toward certain groups of people. These stem from our early socialization and our brains are wired to view certain groups as "foes." The activation in the brain is automatic. But the key is whether we act on those biases and uniformly apply them to anyone from a group. And by honestly acknowledging and understanding them, we can better control and moderate their influence on our interactions.

Here are a few ways to begin the process of being honest with yourself:

- Identify what cultures are most challenging for you. These might include certain national or ethnic cultures but they might also include other types of cultural contexts (e.g., certain age groups, professions, or ideologies). If you had to lead a group coming from a different culture, what culture(s) would stretch you most? Why? Reflecting on these questions and discussing them with trusted colleagues and friends can play a critical role in your becoming more honest with yourself.

- Try some of the implicit association tests available online (http://projectimplicit.org). These tests reveal biases we have toward people's skin color, weight, age, and religion. They're fascinating! They're designed to demonstrate how unconscious bias affects the way we interact with others. And they help promote self-awareness about the automatic impulses we have toward certain cultural groups.

- Revisit assessment results you've received from other inventories you've completed, such as leadership inventories, personality assessments, and emotional competency tools. Look for any trends across these tools and think about how they might influence your cross-cultural interactions. For example, if you see a continual tendency in yourself toward prioritizing task over relationship, consider how that might influence the way you interact in cultures that frustrate you and those that you enjoy most.

If you don't particularly enjoy intercultural interactions and experiences as a whole, owning that is a great start. Then you can begin to think about how to connect things that *do* motivate you with your cross-cultural work. Connect an existing interest with an intercultural component. For example, leaders in the graphic design context can look for what different cultures rate as their favorite logo and seek to understand what that says about the diversity of taste across different cultures. Or leaders in the pharmaceutical industry can learn about the lifestyles and behaviors of patients in various countries to improve the outcome of the research and resulting interventions they release. Runners can explore new terrain as they travel, photographers can capture a diversity of images even within different neighborhoods across the same community, and animal lovers can explore the different wildlife inhabiting the places they visit.

Examine Your Confidence Level

Being honest with ourselves naturally moves us toward another important way to improve CQ Drive: examining our level of confidence in doing cross-cultural work. Self-efficacy is our perception of our ability to successfully reach a goal. It's our degree of confidence in whether we can succeed at a particular task. A great deal of research supports the premise that a leader's level of confidence will critically determine outcomes.[2]

Wendy demonstrated a great deal of self-efficacy as she described the broader goals for her organization. The budget was 300 percent larger than when she came on board five years before and they were helping five times as many children. And she was pretty certain they would continue that kind of growth for the next five years. But the expansion into Central America felt disorienting to Wendy. Her prior experiences and unconscious bias eroded her confidence in working in Central America.

Self-efficacy is an important predictor of cross-cultural adjustment.[3] If you're tentative about working in a particular culture, it will inevitably erode your effectiveness in doing things such as negotiating contracts, managing conflict, and creating new opportunities.[4] Wendy tried to build her confidence by learning everything she could about the culture and the children at risk throughout the region. This is a good starting point for addressing low self-efficacy.[5] In addition, talking to others who have been successful working in the culture, finding someone to be your interpreter and coach along the way, and gaining some small, positive experiences are all ways to improve your self-confidence in cross-cultural work. As Wendy begins to have positive experiences with Hispanic men, and as she reflects on those experiences, she can begin to change her internal bias and lack of confidence in and motivation for adapting to the cultures in Central America.

It's a delicate balance. Too many leaders are overly confident that they'll be fine wherever they go. That's equally detrimental. But sometimes intercultural training and management courses focus so much on the mistakes leaders have made globally that it causes us to be paralyzed by the fear of failure.

For me, looking at my low motivation for and confidence in teaching in Malaysia caused me to spontaneously shift my topic for the day. We were supposed to continue a subject we began the day before: developing succession plans for retiring leaders. I knew I could cover the material, but I lacked confidence that I could get the participants engaged in discussing it beyond what we had already done the previous day. I had recently been thinking a lot about the influence of organizational culture on innovation, and a number of my informal conversations with the seminar participants were related to this topic. So I made a quick judgment call to use the next session to talk about organizational culture and innovation because I felt more confident about doing it with this group. We used a number of group exercises in which I assigned them an organizational culture and suggested a few concrete ways for them to connect the insights that emerged for how they foster ideation. I had to deal with the dissonance this shift in topic created for some participants who wanted to make sure we were going to finish covering the succession planning material promised—a fair concern by any group and accentuated by the cultural values of the participants. But the room felt like it came alive. It might have been the content and topic but it just as well might have been the shift in my personal sense of confidence that this would be something that would better connect and be valuable to them. Our sense of confidence in particular tasks varies based on the situation and context. Growing our confidence will enhance our CQ Drive.

Eat and Socialize

Food is one of the most familiar topics discussed among international travelers. Many business travelers describe the challenge of eating unfamiliar foods and the "scary" experience of being hosted by people who appear insensitive to a visitor's dislike for the local cuisine. Aini, an Indonesian executive, talked with me about the challenges she felt during her first business trip to the United States. She related:

> I still haven't acquired a taste for all the raw greens you North Americans love. Your salads are huge but they're pretty uninviting to me. And having seen the way they package up chicken and freeze it, I can't bring myself to eat the cold chicken often put in the salad. It can't be fresh like the whole ones we get at the markets in Jakarta. When I buy chicken or fish at home, I can see what it looks like before it gets all diced up. But it just turns my stomach to walk through the meat section in the supermarkets in the United States. I just dread mealtime when I'm in the States.

It's ironic to hear Aini describe her distaste for frozen chicken in similar ways to how many North Americans describe the nauseating experience of seeing fresh meat hanging in local markets in other countries. Aini's disgust for some North American foods isn't likely to be as detrimental to her when she's working in the United States as it would be in some other places. For the most part, food is primarily a functional necessity in the dominant North American culture. We eat to work and convenience is king. And if Aini was visiting my home, I'd tell her, "Don't eat anything you don't like." We might feel bad if she didn't eat anything we prepared, but for the most part, we'd want her to pick and choose based on her preferences.

But in many parts of the world, food is deeply rooted in the life of people. Sometimes I've had Indian hosts prepare meals for me that used spices grown on their homestead for hundreds of years. The best Indian meals take days to prepare. So to pass on eating dishes prepared or ordered for you in that context could be far more significant than passing on a dish you just don't care for. It can be seen as an all-out rejection. And as for eating with utensils versus eating with our hands, one of my Indian friends says, "Eating with utensils is like making love through an interpreter!" That says it all when it comes to the affection most Indians have for their cuisine. To reject the food of an Indian colleague can be extremely disrespectful and can erode any possibility of business partnership. Who would have thought food could play such a strong role in successful global performance?

Edwin, a British executive from a Fortune 500 company who often travels to Southeast Asia, observed the huge advantage his love for trying new foods played in his negotiation strategies. Edwin made this commentary when reflecting on his trips to Southeast Asia:

> My hosts are often keen to bring me to places with Western food. They're amazed when I tell them I really want the local food instead. Again and again, they tell me how unusual it is for them to have a Western guest as adventurous as me. Spicy noodles, exotic seafood, fish eyes, frog, snake, insects—I've tried a lot of interesting things. . . . It's at these extended dinner meetings after a long day in the office that the real business transactions happen. I'm convinced this is one of the most important strategies for international business.

Edwin went on to insist that most of the contracts he has negotiated in Southeast Asia happened over shared meals together, not during the formal business meetings during the day. You don't have to be as adventurous as Edwin to gain the value that comes from trying new foods. Making an honest attempt to try something goes a long way. And that's the case whether you are a British leader visiting China or a Chinese leader visiting Britain. When you're willing to try the local cuisine, it has far more value than simply being seen as adventurous. It communicates a willingness to understand and appreciate the culture for what it is. For those who grow queasy thinking about it, here are some strategies you might consider:

- Always try at least a few bites.
- Don't ask what it is. Sometimes the idea makes it seem worse than it actually tastes. Just eat it, with obvious exceptions for food allergies or religious beliefs.
- Slice it thin and swallow quickly.
- If squishy food bothers you, add good amounts of rice, noodles, or bread to firm up the texture.
- Remember that pineapple tempers the bite of hot, spicy foods and Coke makes it burn more. Eat and drink accordingly.
- If you aren't sure *how* to eat it (e.g., with your hands, what to peel off), just ask. Most hosts will love showing you.
- Find something about the food you can compliment and do everything you can to avoid a negative facial expression. You *are* being watched!
- Ask your hosts about any significance the dish might have to them personally or in the culture.

In most cultures, eating together has far more symbolic value than simply "grabbing a bite to eat." Sharing a meal together can often be viewed as a crucial part of building trust. The same can be true in many places when we're invited to do some sightseeing. A Singaporean executive visiting a branch office in Thailand might feel that a ride down the Chao Phraya River in a river taxi is a waste of time. And a Dutch executive might feel that eating the local food with Kenyan bureaucrats has little influence on getting a factory built. But the research demonstrates exactly the opposite. Our level of interest in connecting with the culture and the people as a whole will directly shape how well we do our work in subtle but profound ways. Furthermore, although sightseeing might seem like a waste of time for those from more industrialized, developed countries, in other contexts it demonstrates respect for the history and traditions of a culture and it helps in developing relationships with colleagues in another context. Those coming from more ahistorical cultures often miss the importance of this kind of adaptability.

Cultural differences are more pronounced in social settings than in work settings. A software engineer can often talk "in code" with another information technology expert and immediately find common ground. The same is true between a Brazilian and a German university leader or a Chinese and a Canadian senior manager. Without question, there are challenges and differences in the work environment, but on the whole, we relate more easily with our professional counterparts when talking about work than when we venture into the social context. But many of our work norms are absent once we move into a social setting. Many of the greatest intercultural challenges occur over dinner after leaving the office: What's appropriate conversation? Should I ask about family? Should we discuss work while we eat? What and where should we eat?

As a result, the energy required to socially interact with people from different cultural backgrounds often causes us to retreat to more familiar and comfortable social contexts. Short-term business travelers usually feel more comfortable when traveling with other colleagues from home and eating familiar food. Executives fulfilling an expatriate assignment often cloister themselves in the expat subculture rather than immerse themselves locally. But we're much less likely to succeed in an intercultural setting when we withdraw from it or remain with a large group of colleagues from home. When we come into a new environment together as a group of outsiders, we have a built-in support group and point of identification. As a result, we aren't as motivated to integrate ourselves into the local setting.[6]

This brings us back to the point of being honest with ourselves. It's not that we can never retreat. Introverts, in particular, will quickly become drained by the labor of socializing cross-culturally. And all of us will find occasions, especially when immersed in ongoing, extended work with different cultures, when we need to withdraw for a while, either to spend time with people from a familiar cultural context or to have time alone with some of the comforts of home. I think any business traveler can survive for a few days without McDonald's and Starbucks or rice and tea. But there's a time when tapping into the comforts of home can help sustain the ongoing CQ Drive needed. There's nothing wrong with retreating to recharge our batteries. But if we aren't careful, we could find ourselves progressively drawn away from the local culture. What was meant to be a time of recharging could come at the expense of failing to engage with the local culture.[7] When we look for familiar foods and crave a current copy of our favorite newspaper on our way to a negotiation meeting, we may, as a result, miss out on a huge leveraging opportunity. Think twice before ordering room service and skipping the dinner invitation.

Count the Perks

The fatigue, fears, and anxieties that accompany intercultural work can be overwhelming, but don't be discouraged. There are rewarding payoffs beyond the frequent-flyer miles and souvenirs for friends and family. Reviewing the following proven benefits for culturally intelligent leaders can be helpful in improving low CQ Drive in yourself or others you lead.

Career Advancement

Growing numbers of organizations require that anyone becoming a senior leader must first prove his or her effectiveness working with a multicultural team. Several corporations now require at least two different international assignments in difficult locations before an individual will be considered for an executive-level role.

A study led by INSEAD professor William W. Maddux discovered that an individual's intercultural experiences predicted the number of job offers received, even when controlling for variables such as demographics and personality. Professionals who adapted to and learned about new cultures engaged in job interviews more creatively and demonstrated more openness and initiative. They were seen as being able to bring seemingly unrelated ideas together into meaningful wholes. As a result, these candidates were able to navigate the interview process successfully and received more job offers.[8]

Creativity and Innovation

Learning to negotiate and expand internationally fosters a sense of creativity that can't be gained any other way. The art of negotiation is challenging enough when cultures are shared. But learning how to reach a win-win when dealing with multiple cultural backgrounds grows an overall sense of innovation and creativity that can be applied across many other facets of life and work. It's one thing to understand the cultural differences between German and Chinese cultures. It's quite another to have creatively found a way to develop a working relationship that achieves the respective performance objectives while also demonstrating dignity and honor for one another. There's a correlation between high cultural intelligence and innovation.

Global Networks

As you gain a reputation for culturally intelligent leadership, it expands your professional networks with people around the world. Customers are looking for leaders and companies that understand our diverse world and have existing connections with people and organizations in a variety of places. Leading with cultural intelligence inevitably grows these networks and connections.

Salary, Profitability, and Cost Savings

Given the 70 percent failure rate of international ventures, many organizations are willing to pay for talent who can successfully perform in intercultural situations because it yields higher profits. It doesn't take long to see the benefit to the organization as well as the individual when calculating the cost of a leader who is *ineffective* working across cultures. Consider the following:

- Determine which senior-level leaders have had to deal with the fallout from an unsuccessful cross-cultural venture. What's their pay? Try putting an hourly rate on their time. How many hours have these senior leaders spent dealing with this situation? Just a few meetings a week can equal hundreds of hours. Multiply the number of hours by these leaders' hourly rates.
- Add the cost of other staff who get engaged in it.
- Add the cost of missed opportunities because of all the energy diverted toward this issue.
- Imagine the cost of what this does to the overall morale and future growth of the organization.

Some dismiss cultural intelligence as a lofty ideal and miss its connection to profitability and cost savings. Prioritizing cultural intelligence across an organization has been proven to play a role in increased profitability and cost savings. Subsequently, leaders with high CQ have higher earning potential than those with low CQ. Organizations are waking up to the reality that culturally intelligent leadership is worth the investment. Generously compensating those who do that work well is a helpful way to increase CQ Drive and, more importantly, to better reach your objective.

There are definite perks that come with cross-cultural work. In Part III, we'll look more fully at the return on investment for culturally intelligent leaders and their organizations.

Work for Something Bigger

Although extrinsic motivators such as advancement in your career and salary are valid, at some point, culturally intelligent leaders need to consider something bigger as the ongoing source of motivation for culturally intelligent behavior. Ultimately, a bigger cause is needed to sustain CQ Drive.

John Elkington, dubbed the dean of the corporate social responsibility movement, coined the term *triple bottom line*, meaning businesses need to be equally responsible for people, planet, and profit. He argues that all three are the measure of today's successful organization: Are we causing people suffering, despair, or injustice in the process of making a profit (people)? How does our work affect the environment (planet)? Are we profitable, and if so, what goes along with the profits being made (profits)?[9]

Every organization needs to be fiscally profitable, including nonprofit organizations, which cannot fulfill their mission apart from economic viability. Ironically, the other two bottom lines, environmental responsibility and human welfare, need not conflict with profitability. All three can serve each other. There may be times we give up a profit-producing opportunity because it violates the other two bottom lines. But the emphasis here is more about how we perform and how we use the money earned. Money can be used to offer people opportunity, life sustenance, and empowerment or it can be used to destroy life.[10]

The three bottom lines are indispensable to one another as we tap into a globalized market and workforce. Many companies across the world today realize that success requires earning the respect and confidence of their customers. It's no longer a matter of simply adhering to legal rules and regulations. Whether it's safety standards, child labor practices, or discrimination in hiring, customers are regulating how we do our work.

Elkington's work is an example of what it means to work for something bigger. A deeper, altruistic drive is a far more sustainable motivation for cultural intelligence than merely pursuing global markets for selfish interests. In fact, cultural intelligence cannot exist apart from true care for the world and for people.[11] At the very core of cultural intelligence is the desire to learn with and about other people. So we must beware of penetrating the cultural contexts of other groups and imposing our views of life on them. Instead, our global operations give us a chance to gain mutually beneficial insights and beliefs from transcontinental relationships.

What might a more transcendent motivation look like for leaders from the United States? Perhaps a word of caution is needed here. For several years, there was a sense that a leader from the United States could be welcomed anywhere in the world with our services, products, and ideas. But in recent years, there's been a sea change in attitudes toward the United States and what it means to work with us. International leaders in business, government, and nonprofit organizations whisper behind closed doors about the way visiting Americans live in their own bubbles without having much genuine interaction with their overseas counterparts, much less the locals. One senior foreign policy adviser told Fareed Zakaria of *Newsweek,* "When we meet with American officials, they talk and we listen—we rarely disagree or speak frankly because they simply can't take it in."[12] Kisore Mahbubani, Singapore's former foreign secretary and ambassador to the United Nations, put it this way: "There are two sets of conversations, one with Americans in the room and one without."[13] But as U.S. leaders posture themselves with a spirit of openness, collaboration, and even compromise, not only will it change their one-on-one interactions, but it may also begin to slowly change the global view of the United States.

Leaders from other contexts need to wrestle with a more transcendent motivation as well. As emerging economies such as the BRIC (Brazil, Russia, India, China) and MINT (Mexico, Indonesia, Nigeria, Turkey) nations become more influential, leaders in both the public and private sectors need to consider how to use their growing influence and power to wield good. Leaders from places such as China and Saudi Arabia can readily identify with having been the underdog, and they can draw on that experience to increase their altruistic drive to help others. They might even consider the counterintuitive move of coming alongside leaders in places such as Japan, Germany, and the United States to help them reinvent themselves in this new era of globalization. And as nations such as China rise in prominence, they need to consider how to steward their influence globally. These are far more compelling reasons for cross-cultural effectiveness than merely pursuing self-interests.

The call toward something bigger can play a powerful role in increasing our overall CQ Drive. In fact, perhaps the greatest way for Wendy to enhance her self-efficacy and CQ Drive for her upcoming trip and future work in Central America is to tap into her humanitarian orientation. As CEO of an organization committed to underprivileged children, she cares deeply about the pursuit of fairness and equity for all children. Tapping into her altruistic motivation to help children might be what she needs most to compel her to persevere despite some of the cultural dissonance she anticipates and will likely face. The same is true for Klaus, the

German expatriate in Nairobi. When he no longer views Kenyans as merely the people to use to help his company get ahead, it can help him mitigate some of the fears he and his family have about living in Kenya. As he begins to enjoy the opportunity and wonder of working and relating with Kenyan people, he'll tap into a life-giving discovery.

CQ Drive rests in something bigger than us. The challenge for us as leaders is to see our existence not only in terms of our own interests but ultimately about things larger than us. If more power, wealth, and success are all that drive us, we'll burn out pretty fast. But as we and our organizations use the triple bottom line to fit into things larger than us, join them, and serve them, we can take our role in the big picture and find ourselves with heightened energy for persevering through the hard work of cross-cultural leadership. Life is about things that transcend us.[14]

Conclusion

CQ Drive goes beyond the excitement of traveling to a new place or experimenting with ethnically different foods. It's the persistence required when the novelty wears off and the differences start to chafe at us. We have to move beyond our fear, be willing to take risks, and grow in our ability to perform effectively among people and places that seem more foreign than familiar. Trying new foods, taking in some of the local culture, and persevering through the fatigue of relating cross-culturally offers great benefits.

Although the work of CQ Drive is never really done, at some level, it becomes more familiar and comfortable the more we do it. I don't know that it ever becomes easy, but the benefits of persevering through these challenges are immense, in terms of both how it allows you to accomplish your work-related objectives and the portal it gives you to see the world through different eyes.

CQ DRIVE PRACTICES

1. *Calculate the personal, organizational, and global cost of not prioritizing cultural intelligence.* An honest assessment can quickly motivate you and your team to grow your CQ. Write down some consequences that can occur if you can't lead across cultures. What's at stake?

2. *Connect a cross-cultural project with other interests.* If you aren't naturally motivated to experience different cultures, find a way to connect the project with something that does interest you. If you like art, what artistic expressions can you discover in the respective cultures? If you love sports, discover what sports are hot in those cultures. If you're a foodie, the options are endless. If you eat, drink, and sleep business, use this as a way to learn new business insights.

3. *Accept whatever cross-cultural assignments are available.* Direct experience working in cross-cultural situations—watching others who do it successfully and learning on the job—is one of the most important ways to gain confidence to do it more. Multiple intercultural experiences, work and nonwork, are among the best ways to develop CQ Drive.[15]

4. *Try the local specialties.* Most places around the world are gaining more ethnic diversity in the foods available. Break out of your routine and try new foods. And especially when visiting another place, always try at least a few bites. Slice it thin and swallow quickly if you must. But eat, eat, eat!

5. *Live for something bigger.* We were made for more than working ourselves to death and making money. Some of us will take on causes on a large scale. Others will mentor one business leader and make that person's life better. Cultural intelligence offers a way of making the world a better place.

CHAPTER 4

CQ KNOWLEDGE (PART 1):
KNOW WHAT DIFFERENCES MATTER

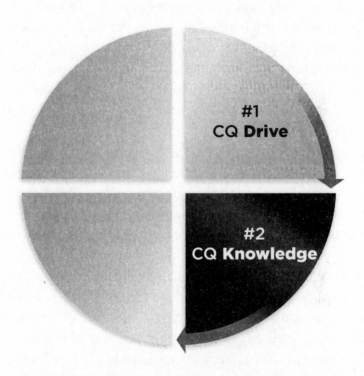

CQ Knowledge: What do I need to know?	
Understanding cultural similarities and differences	
Profile of a leader with high CQ Knowledge	Leaders high in CQ Knowledge have a rich, well-organized understanding of culture and how it affects the way people think and behave. They possess a repertoire of knowledge about how cultures are alike and different. They understand how culture shapes behavior.

"Can we *please* eat something *normal* tonight?!" It's the kind of question I've heard countless times while traveling internationally with people. But this time, the question was coming from my four-year-old daughter! Our family was living in Singapore, and though Western food is readily available there, my wife and I love the local food. Looking straight into my daughter's brilliant blue eyes, I quickly retorted, "Emily. You want something *normal?* You can't get much more *normal* than rice. Do you know how many people eat rice in the world? That's about as *normal* as you can get." Before I could go any further, my wife gave me the *look*. Now was not the time to go off on a cultural intelligence lecture with our kids. But I wanted my daughters to understand that "normal" is relative to our experience.

Ethnocentrism—evaluating other people and their culture by the standards of our own cultural preferences—is found among people everywhere. Seeing the world in light of our own cultural background and experience is inevitable. But ignoring the impact of ethnocentrism on how we lead is the single greatest obstacle to CQ Knowledge.

Most of us tend to underestimate the degree to which we ourselves are a product of culture. It's much easier to see it in others. Emily's question made explicit a guiding assumption for many of us: *My experience is what's normal and best.* Nowadays, Emily and my younger daughter, Grace, enjoy all kinds of spicy, different foods, and they're as quick to catch me in my cultural blind spots as I am them. Grace recently asked me, "Shouldn't CQ mean you show more respect for my love of country music?" Touché.

Is it really such a big deal to think certain kinds of food and music are "normal" and others are "weird"? Maybe and maybe not. But to remain unaware of how culture shapes the way people think and behave is not only foolish, it's expensive. From Fortune 500 businesses to small and medium-side organizations around the world, research consistently demonstrates a high level of failure when expansion into international markets is done without an awareness of how people from other cultures think and behave.

After eight years of struggling in Germany, Wal-Mart sold its eighty-five stores there. Many journalists have theorized about what led to Wal-Mart's failure given its huge success at home, but it's widely agreed that its primary flaw was in ignoring the cultural differences between the United States and Germany. It tried to apply its success formula here in the States to a German market without modifying it. Whether it was the kinds of products offered, the ways items were displayed, the greeters at the entrance, or the policies used in the employee handbook, Wal-Mart's stint in Germany seems to be a case study of what happens when greater attention isn't given to understanding the relevance of cultural differences. As a result, Wal-Mart filed a loss of USD $1 billion because of the failure in Germany and has since become much more adaptive and successful in other overseas markets.[1]

Even if an organization never expands internationally, it's impossible to be an effective leader without having some insight into how culture shapes the thoughts and behaviors of the people touched by your leadership. In fact, Edgar Schein, author of the bestselling book *Organizational Culture and Leadership,* says it's impossible to separate culture and leadership. Schein says cultural norms significantly influence how you define leadership—for example, who should get promoted, what success is, and how to motivate employees. He argues that *creating and managing culture* is all that's really important for leaders. According to Schein, "The unique talent of leaders is their ability to understand and work with culture"—both the organizational and the socio-ethnic cultures they regularly encounter.[2] Don't dismiss cultural understanding as simply politically correct, warm and fuzzy stuff. It will define your leadership.

The ability to understand and work with a culture doesn't just come intuitively. It requires a disciplined effort to better understand cultural differences. CQ Knowledge, the second capability of cultural intelligence, refers to our level of understanding about culture and the ways cultures differ. It's not that leaders with high levels of CQ Knowledge are walking encyclopedias of every culture in the world. That's impossible. Instead, they possess a growing repertoire of knowledge about the macro patterns across cultures. And they can discern when something should be attributed to culture, and when it's more likely a result of something else—such as a personality conflict or power struggle.

In this chapter and the next one, we'll review the most important cultural knowledge you need to lead with cultural intelligence. Our research reveals two subdimensions of CQ Knowledge: cultural-general knowledge, which includes understanding cultural systems, values, and language differences; and context-specific knowledge.[3] Because this is a leadership book, we'll focus on context-specific knowledge about leadership. These subdimensions are the basis of the strategies we'll cover for developing CQ Knowledge. First, we'll learn how to see culture and its role in the way we think, behave, and lead. Next, we'll examine the role of language in how we understand and lead across cultures. Then, we'll review the most relevant cultural systems and values that need to be understood. Finally, we'll examine ten cultural value dimensions. Given the volume of information relevant to CQ Knowledge, the material is divided across two chapters. In this chapter, we'll look at the first three ways to develop CQ Knowledge: (1) see culture's role in yourself and others, (2) understand different languages, and (3) review the basic cultural systems. The fourth element—learn about cultural values—will be discussed in Chapter 5.

HOW TO DEVELOP CQ KNOWLEDGE

1. See culture's role in yourself and others.
2. Understand different languages.
3. Review the basic cultural systems.
4. Learn about cultural values (Chapter 5).

Key Question: What cultural understanding do I need for this cross-cultural assignment?

See Culture's Role in Yourself and Others

The path toward improving CQ Knowledge begins with seeing the influence of culture on everything we think, say, and do. Culture is defined as the beliefs, values, behaviors, customs, and attitudes that distinguish one group from another.[4] Or as some more simply put it, "It's the way we do things around here."

One time my friend Vijay took me to a cricket match in Delhi. I had tried watching cricket before but I was always confused. But Vijay was a great teacher. As we watched the game in the sweltering heat, he started to explain the basic rules, the use of the wickets, the way scoring happened, and the ultimate goal of getting each batsman on the opponent's team out. Not only was the game starting to make sense, I actually felt myself getting drawn into the excitement of the competition. I would have been a sorry sight if I had actually tried to get out on the field and play. But I had a better understanding of what was going on while the cricket pros played their game.

Despite the emphasis of many leadership courses and books on strategic planning and rational decision-making processes, many seasoned executives lead from the gut. As pointed out earlier, this works surprisingly well when leading in a familiar culture. It's not that there's no strategic thinking behind what these executives are doing. Instead, the graduate school of experience has programmed their subconscious to quickly arrive at decisions based on understanding they've gained throughout the years. The challenge comes when a leader relies on that same implicit understanding for making decisions related to different cultures. It might be like a football player jumping in to play cricket assuming they're playing football.

By growing your CQ Knowledge, you can better understand things you may otherwise miss when moving into a new cultural context. This involves understanding the rules, albeit often unspoken, that are behind the behavior and assumptions in a particular culture—whether that's an ethnic group, an organizational culture, or the subculture of a political party or religious group. The objective of the acquired understanding isn't to become like the people in that cultural group or to be able to play their games. The goal is to understand and appreciate the rules behind their lives and society so that you can effectively lead.

Let's consider a few of the different layers of culture we experience as leaders. National culture, such as French or Chinese culture, is the layer of culture that most powerfully shapes behavior. We may not think of ourselves as overly influenced by our national culture until we travel abroad. Then suddenly we find ourselves identifying with other people from our country more than we do when we're home. Though many subcultures exist within most countries, national culture is the cultural orientation that most significantly shapes how most people think and behave.

Next is the influence of different ethnic cultures. I'll repeatedly note the danger of making broad generalizations about all people from a particular country, and this is partly because of the diversity within most domestic contexts—whether it's Zulus and Afrikaans in South Africa; ethnic Chinese, Indians, and Malays in Malaysia; or African Americans and Hispanics in the United States. Most leaders have some consciousness of the ethnic diversity within their own country, but they may need to grow their awareness of the diversity that exists elsewhere. Leaders outside the United States are often perplexed by what appears to be an overly sensitized concern about racism and prejudice in the United States related to the African American subculture. And the very fact that we refer to that subculture as "African American" rather than "black" is confounding to many non-U.S. leaders. But if you're going to be working in the U.S. context, it's important to understand the long history that helps explain the values, behavior, and customs of African Americans compared to the dominant Anglo culture in the United States.

The other culture most consistently encountered by leaders is organizational culture. One of the things I love about my work is the chance to experience so many diverse cultures across different industries and organizations. Spending one day with Coke's executives and the next day with Facebook's can make me feel like I should have had a passport to move from one place to the next—even though I haven't left the country. The same is true when presenting to a group of executives at Samsung as compared to Hyundai. I have to further shift my thinking before presenting to a group of academics and yet again before talking with a group of faith-based leaders. CQ Knowledge includes growing our understanding of the distinct ways organizations celebrate successes, motivate teams, and share their stories.

Each of us is part of several other subcultures, including cultures organized around generational differences, sexual orientation, regions across a country, and religions. Consider the cultures of which you are a part and the ones that most strongly influence how you lead. We aren't merely passive recipients of culture in any of these contexts. Culture isn't something that just happens to us; we're also active creators of it. Many leaders inherit organizational cultures with unhealthy practices and dysfunctional behavior throughout the company. It's extremely challenging to change an organizational culture but it can be done. And we play a role in morphing and adapting the other cultures we belong to as well.[5]

One of leaders' most important roles is to be conscious of how culture shapes their behavior and that of others. Take, for example, Giovanni Bisignani, who recently stepped down from a decade as CEO and director general of the International Air Transportation Association (IATA), the trade association for over 90 percent of commercial airlines globally. One could easily mistake Bisignani's bright-eyed, affable nature as simply that of a nice guy who has had a lot of global experiences. He's one of the warmest people I've ever met. Within seconds of talking to him, he puts you at ease, makes a personal connection, and starts telling stories about tea with Mrs. Gandhi and his favorite travel spots. But this hospitable, gregarious character is a ferociously determined leader who loves a challenge and is relentlessly focused on driving change and bringing about results. The impact of his ten years of leadership at IATA is more than impressive:

- Since 2004, he saved the air industry $54 billion.
- He reformed a dusty, near obsolete organization into the largest Citibank customer in the world.
- He improved the ease by which we travel through e-ticketing, bar-coded boarding passes, and self-service check-in kiosks. More important, he's led air travel to become the safest mode of transportation in the world.
- He built collaborative initiatives between some of the most unlikely partners: competing airlines, democratic presidents and dictators, big guys like Lufthansa and little guys like Air Zimbabwe—just to name a few.
- He moved IATA from being an organization led and dominated by Europeans and North Americans to one in which 60 percent of its members are from developing countries and more than 65 percent of its revenue is from the Middle East and Asia.

Giovanni understood the ubiquitous role of culture in every interaction and negotiation, and as a result, he led monumental change to one of the hardest hit industries of the twenty-first century—the air industry. And he's been a catalyst for some of the most unlikely cross-border collaborations. This is a guy who has dinner with U.S. Secretary of Homeland Security Janet Napolitano one evening and heads off to Iraq the next day to help Iraqi Airways get the airplane parts they need to fly passengers safely. Giovanni's cultural understanding is the compass that gives him the direction he needs when stepping into any meeting.

Not every leader is as convinced as Giovanni about the relevance of cultural understanding. Jeff, a U.S. sales manager from a billion-dollar manufacturing company, talked to me a week before making his second business trip to China to visit a couple of factories in Guangzhou.

Jeff was very animated as we talked. With his legs constantly moving up and down and his fingers nervously tapping on the table, he said, "Okay, no offense. But doesn't this whole cultural thing get a little overplayed? I mean, people are people and business is business. I'll probably have to eat some weird food next week, but otherwise, I don't see what the big differences are."

I resisted jumping in for the moment and listened as Jeff carried on with his line of reasoning. Continuing with what seemed like a lot of nervous energy, Jeff said:

> The way I see it, everyone is just trying to find a way to make a decent living and get ahead in life. I don't care whether you're Chinese, Mexican, or American, people are pretty much the same everywhere. They care about their kids, like you and me. They know you have to be aggressive to survive in this global market. And everyone wants to get ahead. The marketing strategy might need to adapt a little bit, but I think manufacturing is manufacturing and selling is selling wherever you go. Either you're cut out for it or not!

If you only travel to major cities, stay in global hotel chains, and interact with locals who have been trained how to serve international travelers, it's easy to believe the world is pretty much the same everywhere. And there's some merit to Jeff's point that all people share some basic universal characteristics. But the way we express and approach those universal characteristics varies widely across cultural and individual differences. A leader's ability to distinguish between what's universal, what's cultural, and what's personal is one of the most important indicators of cultural intelligence. This discernment stems from growing your CQ Knowledge. As you gain a better understanding of cultural norms, you know whether you're experiencing something that is unique to an individual or typical of most individuals from the culture involved.

The iceberg is a familiar metaphor used when talking about the powerful influence of culture (see Figure 4-1). In my version of this metaphor, I place the universals shared across all humanity at the tip of the iceberg. As Jeff noted, there are a few universals that are true for most everyone and these are things we can readily see. But when you go a bit deeper, you find a slew of differences attributable to varying cultures and individual personalities. This is an important point of understanding. We'll refer back to these three categories of human behavior (universal, cultural, and personal) throughout the book, but here's a brief explanation.

Universal

I love to sit in a busy train station or shopping center and watch all the people. Even in a faraway place where I don't know anyone, I can feel a level of connection simply by watching what appears to be a father with his children, a fellow traveler with her bags, or a couple laughing together. I relate to all these things. We share basic human needs. And emotions such as fear, joy, and disappointment are common to everyone. Acknowledging what we have in com-

Figure 4-1. Three Categories of Human Behavior

UNIVERSAL

CULTURAL

Cultural Artifacts and
Systems
Art, clothing, food, money,
customs, gestures, etc.

Cultural Values and
Assumptions
Unconscious, taken-for-
granted beliefs, percep-
tions, and feelings

PERSONAL

mon can be the first step toward making the foreign seem more familiar. But it's only the tip of the iceberg.

Cultural

If I sit in a train station and watch a stranger with his kids, I can experience a form of connection as a dad, but if I make assumptions about what their relationship should look like, I've moved into questionable territory. Or to use the earlier analogy, interpreting cricket using the rules of football would lead to misunderstanding and confusion. I might *think* I understand and be entirely wrong.

As noted in Figure 4-1, certain aspects of a culture are visible. The way people drive, the local currency, religious symbols, or the way a business images itself are things that can be observed and identified. These are the visible cues about cultural differences that exist in any culture. But the most important points of understanding are the beliefs, values, and assumptions that lie beneath the surface of what's visible. As represented by the iceberg, beneath the surface are the beliefs, values, and assumptions that drive behavior.

If Jeff fails to see the profound differences between the way a Chinese business partner and an American one thinks and behaves, he's sure to hit all kinds of roadblocks and will unlikely see lasting success working cross-culturally. Ignorance about the cultural differences that abound in the multicultural workforce around us puts us on the pathway toward ineffective, irrelevant leadership.

Consider the Chinese concept of *guanxi* as an example of why Jeff needs to realize that a "people are people" approach is an insufficient rule of thumb for guiding his interactions in China. *Guanxi* refers to the connections and resulting obligations between two individuals. It exists between Chinese families first and foremost, but it's also found among classmates and professional colleagues because of a shared history together. When adopting *guanxi*, individuals loosely keep track of the favors given and the debts owed between one another. Given the underlying presence of *guanxi* in most Chinese relationships, Jeff would be wise to learn the significance of the gifts his colleagues in Guangzhou may give him as a way to establish and build a relationship together. The same actions done at home might appear to be bribery or little more than just a token gesture. But misunderstanding what this means in China could derail everything Jeff was sent there to do.

Talk to most anyone who has worked on getting a deal in China and he will tell you stories about people who insisted on getting him drunk. In a culture where *guanxi* can make or break you in business, getting drunk with a potential business partner is often viewed as a crucial way of solidifying that relationship and showing that you are, in fact, friends. First, business dinners usually start with an invitation. Typically, the person doing the inviting should be of at least the same leadership level as the person being invited. Furthermore, the person doing the inviting pays for dinner. Chinese individuals who follow more traditional norms will make the dinner invitation in person or by phone, not by email or text message. Email is considered too impersonal, and it allows a tangible record of those with whom you do business.

Unlike during most Western business dinners, business itself is usually the least talked about topic during a Chinese business dinner. If anything, it's saved for a sliver of time at the end of dinner, although at that point, most of the people involved are so drunk that no real business decisions can come out of it. But don't think this means it's a waste of time. The point of the dinner is to solidify relationships. It's a big part of determining whether you're trustworthy and to see how you behave when you aren't sober enough to filter what you say. Expect personal questions and don't be afraid to talk about your personal life. And if you keep drinking, it will be seen as a symbol of friendship. The more you drink, the more pleased your cohorts will be, because it shows you're willing to get drunk with them, just like you would with your friends. The Chinese believe that drinking together deepens and strengthens friendships because it loosens people up and helps relieve misunderstanding, no matter how tense the situation might be. Granted, there are certainly times when excessive drinking will be used to wear you down. But the primary orientation behind this practice is social.

If Jeff assumes that going out for dinner and drinks is optional, similar to what it might mean in many other cultural contexts, he can be blindsided. There may be health or religious reasons why Jeff decides he can't fully participate in this drinking scene. But he at least needs to make that decision being consciously aware of the meaning behind it. We'll further address how to use this kind of cultural understanding to effectively lead when we get to CQ Strategy and CQ Action.

For now, the point is to see the relevance of cultural differences to how we lead and do business. A former U.S. ambassador to Yemen and the United Arab Emirates told me that during his career he had witnessed a continual stream of U.S. salespeople moving in and out of the Persian Gulf to sell their goods and services. All too often he saw North American sales reps losing opportunities to their British, French, or Japanese counterparts because they tried to use the same sales pitch from home in the Middle East. Meanwhile, their counterparts from other countries spent more time learning about the local culture and even the local language. As a result, they secured contracts lost by the North Americans. This might not be any more true of North American sales reps than sales reps from other countries but the point is that learning about cultural markets has a direct connection to generating sales.[6]

Culture is everywhere. It shapes how you lead and it influences how others perceive your leadership. As you better understand the relevance of culture, you'll be much better equipped to assess situations and make decisions that are appropriate for your organization and the individuals involved.

Personal

At the deepest level of the iceberg are individual differences. Leaders functioning at the highest levels of cultural intelligence are able to see when the behavior of others is a reflection of their cultural background and when it's idiosyncratic behavior from one individual. There are ways I behave that are consistent with how most North American men behave. I'm task-oriented, independent, and I prefer clear, explicit communication. And there are characteristics of me that would be unfair to generalize to other North American men, including my insatiable wanderlust and the intensity with which I approach most anything I do. A culturally intelligent leader will learn to identify the personal quirks and characteristics of individuals versus those that fit cultural norms. The best way to do so is by understanding cultural systems and values—something explained later in this chapter and the next. By learning these broad cultural norms, you have a way of knowing whether a behavior is consistent with cultural tendencies or idiosyncratic.

A recent study asked people in seventy-two nations to share their predominant images of the United States. The winners: war and *Baywatch!*[7] In a post-9/11 era, it takes little guessing to figure out why many people in the world equate the United States with war. As for *Baywatch*, it's the most exported U.S. television program in the world, quickly being crowded out by *Friends,* which is now in syndication every hour of the day somewhere in the world.[8]

Many of my U.S. friends are very conflicted about our military interventions, and I don't know many Americans who watch, much less like, the characters on *Baywatch*. But that doesn't change the fact that some people will make assumptions about people from the United States that are entirely off base. And the same thing happens everywhere. Not all Chinese leaders want to take people drinking and not all Millennials are looking for flexible work schedules.

The reverse is also problematic—that is, observing an individual's behavior and generalizing it to an entire culture. One Canadian leader who managed a Sikh Indian employee told me, "One of the things I've noticed about Sikhs is they don't like to travel. Every time I ask Mr. Singh to attend a meeting out of town, he comes up with an excuse." When I asked her whether she had observed this among other Sikh employees, she said Mr. Singh was the first Sikh she'd hired. But she had assumed it was a cultural thing because who wouldn't want to get out of London, Ontario, every once in a while at the company's expense. She presumed any unfamiliar, inexplicable behavior she observed must have been related to his cultural background.

Later, we'll note the value of using cultural norms and values as a starting point for understanding others. But caution is always needed. Cultural intelligence is required to discern between what's universal, what's cultural, and what's personal. Once we understand the impact of culture, we're ready to understand the middle layer of the iceberg: languages, cultural systems, and cultural value orientations.

Understand Different Languages

A few years ago, the Dairy Association led a wildly successful marketing campaign throughout the United States built on the slogan "Got Milk?" Unfortunately, when the campaign was exported to Mexico, the translation read, "Are you lactating?"[9] There are countless other examples like this. A U.S. software company suffered from having the name of its industry translated as "underwear" when launching internationally. A European company couldn't succeed selling its chocolate and fruit dessert called "Zit" in the United States nor could the Finns who attempted to sell "Super Piss," a Finnish product for unfreezing car door locks. These examples are humorous but the challenge of language goes beyond funny translations. Microsoft experienced a great deal of resistance from many regions around the world in response to its icon "My Computer," which assumed everyone owned his or her own computer. And Microsoft's "mail" and "trash" icons looked nothing like the mailboxes and trash bins used in most places globally.[10]

Read almost any book on effective leadership, and you'll learn about the essential role of consistent, clear communication. Clarity is one of the universal leadership skills desired by followers from all cultures.[11] And communication, whether creating a marketing campaign, drafting a memo, or casting a vision, is ubiquitously tied to culture. Some say language and culture are one and the same, pointing to the reality that Eskimos have several different words for snow and very few to describe tropical fruits. The reverse is true in some tropical contexts. Language and culture evolve together as people live in relationship to their surroundings. As we grow in

CQ Knowledge, we need to understand some basics about communication and language and their relationship to culture.

Some flippantly quip, "English is becoming the lingua franca of international business." But in actuality, English is just one of the major languages of world trade and the mother tongue of only 5 percent of the world's population.[12] Leaders who speak more than one language have an advantage over those who don't because when you're fluent in a language, speaking and *thinking* in that language becomes an automatic, subconscious action. Not only can we more easily communicate with others who speak that language, we also gain a heightened ability to see how they label the world. It provides a way to understand what's going on that is much harder to grasp when done through translation. Jaguar, the British automobile maker, discovered the importance of language when it began in-house German-language studies to help increase its competitiveness in Germany against Mercedes and BMW. A year after doing so, Jaguar's sales in Germany jumped 60 percent.[13]

If you speak only one language, consider signing up for an introductory course or hiring a tutor to learn a foreign language. Chances are, you won't have to look far to find someone who can teach you the basics. Or you could get a Skype "pen pal" with whom you can regularly communicate in another language for free. While becoming fluent is a great ideal, just the process of learning another language significantly contributes to growth in CQ Knowledge. You might find yourself innovating and leading in new ways simply as a result of learning a new language. And being able to say even a few words in a counterpart's native tongue speaks volumes.

Language understanding can be an issue even when working within another English-speaking context. Different expressions and terms are frequent points of confusion among North Americans, Brits, Indians, and Australians.

Similar communication challenges exist when moving from one organization or profession to the next. An academic talking with a group of business executives needs to translate academic terms into words that communicate effectively in the corporate context. I often encounter people who work in professional cultures that are unfamiliar to me, such as medical professionals, biochemists, or automotive manufacturers. I immediately observe the difference between the cultural intelligence of those individuals who can talk to me about their work using language I understand versus others who use all kinds of trade lingo that means nothing to me. Doctors and nurses with CQ Knowledge have to adjust their verbal and nonverbal language when talking about a diagnosis with family members versus doing so with medical peers. With CQ Knowledge, we understand that our words stem from a variety of the cultural contexts that shape who we are.

I chair the board of a nonprofit organization. This nonprofit was extremely successful during the first seven years of its existence. But then for the next three years its activity and bottom line began a steady decline. One of the things a consultant observed in talking with several of the staff and constituents was an unusual aversion toward anything that sounded "corporate" or institutional. In fact, one business leader who observed this nonprofit described the organizational culture as having antibodies in its system toward anything that sounded remotely corporate. Our board was in the midst of seeking a new leader for the organization, and part of applying cultural intelligence was to change the title of the primary leader from CEO to team leader. Of course, if the sole change made was in the title on the job description, the aversion toward corporate culture would be addressed only momentarily. But this shift in language was the first step toward developing a leadership plan that uniquely suited the culture of the organization, expressed in a language that resonated with its members rather than just mimicking titles and structures from other places.

Communicating, both formally and informally, is perhaps the most important thing a leader does. Many of the problems that occur in an organization are the direct result of people failing to communicate in ways that truly enhance understanding. Learning appropriate language for a cultural context provides the understanding necessary for adapting the way we communicate, something we'll revisit when looking at the fourth CQ capability, CQ Action.

Review the Basic Cultural Systems

Another important part of understanding different cultures is to learn about different cultural systems. Cultural systems are the ways a society has organized itself in terms of meeting basic needs and the structures required for order. Without careful observation, the significance of these systems can easily be missed. There are six cultural systems that are most relevant for leaders: economic, marriage and family, educational, legal and political, religious, and artistic.

Economic Systems: Capitalist vs. Socialist

Every society has to come up with basic ways of meeting its members' universal needs of food, water, clothing, and housing. Understanding how a culture has organized itself to produce, allocate, and distribute these basic resources is extremely important to culturally intelligent leadership. Most of us are pretty familiar with the two most predominant economic systems today—capitalism and socialism (Table 4-1)—though most economic systems are a mix of the two.

Capitalism, found in places like the United States and Singapore, is based on the principle of individuals gaining resources and services based on their capacity to pay for them. The assumption underlying capitalism is that individuals are motivated to care for themselves and the market exists to meet their needs. Competition is seen as good for the consumer and thus for the whole.

On the other end of the continuum is socialism, found in places like Denmark and New Zealand. The state plays a much more active role in the production and distribution of basic resources by ensuring some equality of access for everyone in society to basic resources. Most of us have strong opinions about which system is superior, but we must beware of assuming there's only one right way to distribute goods and services. There is a wide range of other possibilities for how cultures address economic needs, particularly in more tribal contexts. You don't need to be an expert on how the entire economic system works in every culture; but a general awareness of the differing ways in which economic systems are organized will enhance your ability to negotiate and develop a working relationship outside your home culture. Table 4-1 offers you a few ways to begin thinking about the leadership implications of these cultural differences.

Marriage and Family Systems: Kinship vs. Nuclear Family

Each society works out a system for who can marry whom, under what conditions, and according to what procedures. A related system of child care becomes standardized in most cultures. The most commonly described family systems are kinship systems and nuclear-family systems (Table 4-2). Most of the world is organized around kinship-based societies in which blood relationship and solidarity within one's family and clan is central. For example, a Chinese philanthropist is likely to be more concerned about giving in a way that benefits his or her family and heirs than to making a pledge with Bill Gates and Warren Buffett. Or a Middle Eastern executive is more likely to do business with someone who knows his family or has some previous connections to his family than with someone who has impressive credentials. This is called *con-*

Table 4-1. Economic Systems

Economic Systems
The basic ways a society organizes itself to meet its members' universal needs of food, water, clothing, and housing.

Capitalism	Socialism
A society created around the idea of individuals gaining resources and services based on their capacity to pay for them. Decisions are market driven.	A society in which the state coordinates and implements the production and distribution of basic resources through central planning and control.

Leadership Implications
• Consider how best to motivate personnel in light of the predominant economic system. Competition tends to be a better motivational strategy in capitalist societies and cooperation in socialist ones.   • Understand which industries in a particular place are state run and which are privatized. And be aware that even some privatized companies have heavy state-level investment.   • When expanding your organization into a country with a different economic system, consider what human resources policies will need to be revised in light of the way health care and retirement is done, how to do performance reviews, and appropriate compensation.

sanguine kinship, in which identity rests most in how individuals are genealogically connected. Kinship societies are made up of extended families in which the household often includes three or more generations. Even corporate leaders in kinship cultures like South Africa or Oman will often spend time trying to determine one's genealogical connections as part of a first encounter.

In contrast, the nuclear-family system, sometimes called *affinal kinship*, is found more predominantly in the Western world and among the middle class. It is usually based on two generations whose group members are related by marriage. *Family* refers to parents and children, and, essentially, it dissolves with the death of a spouse. Societies based on nuclear families are those where employees are much more apt to pick up and move when a better career opportunity comes along. And the identity of individuals

Table 4-2. Family Systems

Family Systems
The system a society develops for who can marry whom and the arrangements for how children and senior members are cared for.

Kinship Family	Nuclear Family
The family finds its identity in several generations of history and the household often includes three or more generations.	The family is based on two generations whose members are related by marriage and consists primarily of parents and children.

Leadership Implications
• Expect introductions in kinship societies to be embedded with references to siblings, uncles, parents and grandparents, etc. Learning about the career of an individual's parent may be very important. In contrast, introductions in nuclear-family societies are usually focused on one's vocational role and what one does for the organization. Conversations about family are considered "personal" and only appropriate after getting to know one another a bit better. • When leaders from nuclear-family systems work with colleagues and employees from kinship family systems, keep in mind that allowing room for family obligations will be important when recruiting and retaining talent from kinship societies. • When leaders from kinship family systems work with colleagues and employees from nuclear-family systems, beware that they may not see the importance of hearing or sharing about extended-family relationships during an initial introduction.

in these societies is more typically derived from one's immediate family and one's vocation rather than the heritage of one's extended family. Nuclear-family systems place a great deal of value on parent-child relationships, husband-and-wife relationships, and sibling relationships. Family systems play a profound role in the choices employees make and the things that motivate potential markets.

Understanding the colliding approaches to family life is becoming increasingly relevant to how we lead. As elderly parents are living longer and as more men take on responsibility caring for children, understanding a culture's approach to family is critical. In fact, the family system is widely regarded as the single most important cultural system leaders need to understand; but this information often feels irrelevant to some leaders.[14] Consider why some basic knowledge of these kinds of differences would help a Western leader trying to negotiate a contract with a business owned by an ethnic Chinese family. Many of the most successful firms in cities like Beijing, Jakarta, Kuala Lumpur, and Singapore are run by ethnic Chinese leaders who reflect a kinship approach to business. These companies are typically managed by the patriarch of the family, who leads with unquestioned authority and is aided by a small group of family members and close subordinates. When the owner retires, the firm is typically passed to the next generation. These companies rarely relinquish control to outsiders and they usually put only family members on the board of directors.[15] Or for multinational companies working in Middle Eastern contexts, it would be beneficial to consider the importance of working with local contractors who are connected to a local sheik's family or donating funds for a sheik's family village in order to gain the sheik's cooperation and approval. Family systems are an extremely relevant issue for how you lead across borders. The material in Table 4-2 will help you consider this further.

Educational Systems: Formal vs. Informal

Societies develop patterns for how their senior members transmit their values, beliefs, and behaviors to their offspring. This is at the core of how societies develop systems for educating and socializing their young (Table 4-3). Most of the world today is moving toward more formalized education in which young people are taught through schools, books, and professional teachers. But even in many developed cultures, such as South Africa, Israel, or Japan, informal education from one's senior family members is seen as critically important alongside the priority of rigorous, formal education in these places. And the use of rote teaching in which students are expected to recite information taught versus

Table 4-3. Educational Systems

Eduational Systems	
The patterns for how the senior members of a culture transmit their values, beliefs, and behaviors to their offspring.	
Formal The use of schools, books, and professionally trained teachers to educate youth.	**Informal** The emphasis of wisdom passed to youth from extended-family members, parents, and siblings.
Leadership Implications	
• Develop and adapt training programs for employees with an understanding of the educational systems and preferences of people in different cultures. Some teaching methods may be very foreign or uncomfortable to individuals from certain cultures. • Seek to understand the extent to which formal, academic research is valued as compared to conventional wisdom in the ways you motivate, negotiate, and market your work. • When seeking to debunk a myth or advance a new idea, understand the primary source of socialization in a culture (e.g., sage wisdom versus academic research).	

the development of analytical skills is an important difference among many educational approaches. If you play a role in designing training, consider how the varied educational perspectives and experiences will shape how participants respond and learn. Think carefully about the age of the person you send to conduct training in a context where people expect teachers to be more senior.

Leaders coming from Asia are often frustrated with the perceived limitations among Westerners for memorizing and retaining information. They see Westerners as struggling to synthesize individual parts into a whole. Western leaders experience the same frustration when their attempts at analysis are met with resistance from Eastern counterparts. An understanding of the educational system and approach to learning used by a culture will enhance the way you conduct meetings; develop partnerships; and market, train, and develop personnel.

Legal and Political Systems: Formal vs. Informal Governance

Most cultures develop systems for maintaining order to ensure citizens will not violate the rights of others in the society. This results in the legal system of a society, which is closely tied with the government of a particular place. In places like the United States, there's a formal legal system governed by a written constitution and through local, state, and federal laws. Although less formalized and complex, many smaller-scale, technologically simple societies also have effective ways of controlling behaviors (Table 4-4).

Because many businesses lack knowledge of how the governing system works in a new place, they become extremely frustrated when it comes to maintaining good working relationships among employees and with local officials. One of the greatest mistakes made by leaders as they move in and out of various countries is assuming the government system works pretty much like it does at home. Another typical response is assuming a legal system is corrupt or inferior because it's different. Understanding and respecting a society's legal system will significantly enhance the ability to work effectively in that culture.

It's also important to be aware that there are often variations even within a nation's given legal system. For example, China has universal laws that govern the country, but there are numerous issues that are governed by individual provinces and cities. Many other countries have similar variations among different districts, provinces, and regions. In some contexts, laws apply differently to different ethnic groups within a society. Malaysia, an Islamic state, has a different set of standards for its indigenous Malay citizens than it does for citizens of Chinese or Indian descent. One U.S. company operating in Kuala Lumpur began offering yoga classes for employees during the lunch hour. The class was led by a North American instructor as a way to offer employees holistic exercise. There was enthusiastic participation from several of the Indian and Chinese personnel. But no Malays, the predominant population in the country, ever came to yoga. Eventually the company learned that it's illegal for Malays to practice yoga because yoga is believed to incorporate elements of Hinduism, which could corrupt a Muslim's faith. Complete understanding of all the specific legal structures is not necessary, but an appreciation for the significance of how a legal system affects the way we work in different contexts is essential. The suggestions in Table 4-4 will help you get started.

Religious Systems: Rational vs. Mystical

Why do bad things happen to good people? How come drunk drivers survive while innocent people get killed? Why do tsunamis kill some innocent people while others escape?

Every culture develops a way of explaining what otherwise seems inexplicable. There are no uniform conventions for answering these questions, but all societies offer a variety of supernatural and religious beliefs for things that go beyond human understand-

Table 4-4. Legal Systems

Legal Systems	
The systems developed by a society to protect citizens' rights.	
Formal A very formalized system that is chronicled in things such as a written constitution and laws.	**Informal** Although less formalized, simple legal systems are still binding and are passed along through conventional wisdom. Citizens and visitors are presumed to understand and follow the rules.
Leadership Implications	
• Recruit local expertise to aid you in negotiating with legal and government officials. • Take the time to learn which laws are relevant for your work in a respective place. • Find out what unwritten practices should be used or avoided with legal officials. For example, giving a gift to a government official will be essential in some cultures and can get you arrested in another.	

ing. Admittedly, there are many differences within most cultures for how different individuals and their religions answer questions like these. One of the distinguishing differences between how many cultures organize their supernatural belief systems is rooted in the extent to which they take a rational, scientific approach to answering the inexplicable versus a more spiritual and mystical outlook on life. The rational approach puts more emphasis on individual responsibility and work ethic whereas the mystical way places a higher degree of confidence in supernatural powers, both good and evil (Table 4-5).

Religious and supernatural beliefs can shape work-related attitudes in profound ways. Max Weber, often called the founder of

Table 4-5. Religious Systems

Religious Systems
The ways a culture explains the supernatural and what otherwise seems inexplicable.

Rational	Mystical
The emphasis is on finding reason-based scientific answers to the supernatural with a focus on individual responsibility and work ethic.	The emphasis is on supernatural powers, both good and evil, that control day-to-day events and life.

Leadership Implications
• Be respectful about how you discuss your religious beliefs and learn what might be most likely to offend someone in light of his or her religious beliefs. Be alert to the most potentially offensive things that could be done in regard to a culture's religious beliefs and seek to avoid those practices. • Become a student of how religious values and supernatural beliefs affect the financial, management, and marketing decisions made by organizations in a particular culture. • Find out key religious dates. Avoid opening a new business in China during the Festival of the Dead or on Deepavali in India. And don't schedule an important meeting on days such as Christmas or Chinese New Year.

sociology, analyzed the relationship between Protestantism and capitalism. Capitalism is partially driven by a Protestant work ethic, which is prevalent in Western societies and emphasizes hard work, diligence, and frugality with the aim of accumulating capital. It's assumed this approach will be the best for society. The guiding thought is: *A society won't survive without expecting people to work hard for it.*[16]

In contrast, Islam emphasizes charity to the poor and has rigorous measures to ensure profitable gains don't come at the expense of the poor. As a result, most Islamic banks prohibit charging interest on loans because gains from loans are seen as exploitive gains from the poor. Innovative businesses working in the Islamic context have factored in this reality by charging a fee up front rather than charging interest. Non-Islamic companies working in Islamic countries need to have a basic understanding of these Islamic practices.[17]

One French business opened its Thailand office one flight above a statue of Buddha. Only after several months of virtually no business did this company learn that no one was coming to the office because it was violating a sacred rule: Never put yourself above Buddha, literally! After moving to a new location, business took off. Elsewhere, a Japanese multinational corporation was caught off guard by the extent to which religious beliefs affected its global expansion. The company decided to build a factory on a piece of land in rural Malaysia that was formerly a burial ground of the aboriginal people who had lived in the region. After the factory was built, mass hysteria resulted among the factory workers of Malay origin. Many employees claimed they were being possessed by spirits. They believed that erecting the factory on the former burial ground had disturbed the spirits, causing them to swarm the factory premises.[18]

We can't underestimate the powerful role of religious beliefs and practices in how we work in different places. For Western leaders, who are often perceived to be Christian even if they aren't, conversing about some of the other great religions of the world will demonstrate significant respect when interacting with leaders from other parts of the globe. Those coming from religiously devout contexts into more secular ones need to understand the perceptions that may be associated with religious devotion. You need not abandon your own religious convictions or pretend to have them in order to convey honor and appreciation for the views and practices of others. This is a significant point to understand about cultural intelligence. Cultural intelligence doesn't mean abandoning our convictions, values, and assumptions. Instead, we're seeking to understand and respect the beliefs and priorities of others and express our own values and beliefs in ways that are appropriate, respectful, and effective.

Artistic Systems: Solid vs. Fluid

Finally, every society develops a system of aesthetic standards that gets manifested in everything from decorative art, music, and dance to the architecture and planning of buildings and communities. There are many different ways we could examine artistic systems. One way of thinking about it is to observe the extent to which a society's aesthetics reflect clear lines and solid boundaries versus more fluid ones. Many Western cultures favor clean, tight boundaries, whereas many Eastern cultures prefer more fluid, indiscriminate lines (Table 4-6).

In most Western homes, kitchen drawers are organized so that forks are with forks and knives are with knives. The walls of a room are usually uniform in color, and when there is a creative shift in color, it usually happens at a corner or along a straight line midway down a wall. Pictures are framed with straight edges, molding covers up seams in the wall, and lawns are edged to form a clear line between the sidewalk and the lawn. Why? Because Westerners view life in terms of classifications, categories, and taxonomies. And cleanliness itself is largely defined by the degree of order that exists. It has little to do with sanitation and far more to do with whether things appear to be in their proper place.

Maintaining boundaries is essential in the Western world; otherwise, categories begin to disintegrate and chaos sets in.[19] Most Westerners want dandelion-free lawns and roads with clear lanes prescribing where to drive and where not to drive. Men wear a tie to cover the adjoining fabric on the shirt they put on before going to a symphony, where they listen to classical music based on a scale with seven notes and five half steps. Each note has a fixed pitch, defined in terms of the lengths of the sound waves it produces.[20] A good performance occurs when the musicians hit the notes precisely.

In contrast, many Eastern cultures have little concern in everyday life for sharp boundaries and uniform categories. Different colors of paint may be used at various places on the same wall. And the paint may "spill" over onto the window glass and ceiling. Meals

Table 4-6. Artistic Systems

Artistic Systems
A society's approach to aesthetics including decorative art, music, architecture, web design, and city planning.

Solid	Fluid
A preference for clean, tight boundaries that emphasize precision and straight lines.	A preference for more fluid, indiscriminate lines with an emphasis on ebb and flow and flexibility.

Leadership Implications

- Determine whether you need to alter the color schemes, navigation logic, and representations on your website for various regions. What might seem like a clear navigation approach in your culture might be very confusing in another place.

- Beware of assuming that symbols or logos can be universally applied in all cultural contexts. Do your homework to find out how symbols will be received in the places where you work.

- Learn what cultural icons are revered. For example, inappropriate use of lions or the Great Wall when marketing to Chinese will erode credibility.

are a fascinating array of ingredients where food is best enjoyed when mixed together on your plate or, just as likely, on a communal plate. Roads and driving patterns are flexible. The lanes ebb and flow as needed depending on the volume of traffic. In a place like Cambodia or Nigeria, the road space is available for whichever direction a vehicle needs it most, whatever the time of day. And people often meander along the road in their vehicles the same way they walk along a path.

There are many other ways aesthetics between one place and another could be contrasted. But consistent with the CQ model, the important point is a basic understanding of how cultures differ within the realm of aesthetics. Soak in the local art of a place and chalk it up to informing your strategy for international business. When designing a website, beware of how culturally bound color, navigation, and symbols are. Do more than simply translate the words of a brochure or instructional guidebook. Consider how the layout and design may need to be adjusted. It's unrealistic to come up with a different version of every document for every culture reflected in today's global organization. But careful thinking about the role of culture in how people will understand and react to design and aesthetics is essential. Use the suggestions in Table 4-6 to consider how this relates to your team.

Understanding these basic cultural systems and some overarching ways they function across various cultures is a key part of developing your CQ Knowledge. It's easy to overlook the importance and relevance of these systems if we don't take time to consider them. And as demonstrated in the iceberg metaphor (see Figure 4-1), there will always be individuals within a culture who stray from the cultural norms for aesthetics or any of these cultural systems.

Conclusion

CQ Knowledge begins with understanding culture's role in people's thoughts, attitudes, and behaviors. It's a matter of discerning what's universal to all humans, what's attributable to specific cultures, and what's idiosyncratic to individuals. Then we need to understand the role of language in culture and gain a basic grasp of the systems developed by cultures to deal with economics, family, education, legal issues, religion, and artistic expression. In the next chapter, we'll look at one more crucial aspect of CQ Knowledge: understanding ten cultural dimensions used to compare cultures.

CHAPTER 5

CQ KNOWLEDGE (PART 2): UNDERSTAND TEN CULTURAL VALUE DIMENSIONS

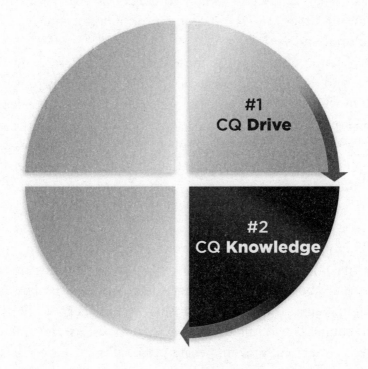

The journey toward leading with cultural intelligence continues. As described in Chapter 4, CQ Knowledge is your level of understanding about culture and the ways cultures differ. Chapter 4 reviewed three ways to develop CQ Knowledge: (1) See culture's role in yourself and others, (2) understand different languages, and (3) review the basic cultural systems. This chapter explains one more important dimension of building and applying CQ Knowledge: Learn about cultural values.

You'll undoubtedly see a connection between what a culture values and the cultural systems (e.g., economic, aesthetic, legal) reviewed in Chapter 4. Cultural values are what get emphasized most when teaching people about cross-cultural leadership. How do people in Mexico approach time or authority compared with people in Germany? Although cultural values are only one dimension of what you need to know to effectively lead with cultural intelligence, they are a significant part of building your repertoire of cultural understanding.

Given the abundance of books devoted to describing these values and the norms for various cultures,[1] I've simply provided a brief overview of ten of these cultural value dimensions to demonstrate how they connect with our research on CQ. All of the usual cautions against stereotyping apply here. It's dangerous to assume that all Norwegians are direct or that all Koreans prefer hierarchical leaders. And it's never appropriate to describe an entire cultural group with negative, judgmental descriptions, such as "___ people are all lazy and corrupt."

As long as we remain open to expecting variability among different people from the same culture (e.g., some Latinos are more concerned about punctuality than others), using cultural norms as a best first guess is worthwhile for shaping initial expectations and interactions. This is one of the best ways to discern the difference between what's cultural and what's personal (see Figure 4-1).

Individualism vs. Collectivism

My oldest daughter is in the midst of deciding what university to attend. My wife and I are guiding her on things we want her to consider, but, ultimately, where she goes will be *her* decision. This is the individualist way: teaching kids from an early age to make choices, be responsible for themselves, and pursue their dreams.

Some of our friends from more collectivist cultures can't fathom that we won't tell Emily where to go. The collectivist way is for parents to strongly influence where a child goes to university and to make that choice in light of what will be best for the entire family.

Individualism versus collectivism is, at its core, a difference in identity. From an individualist perspective, if a decision affects you, you should be the one to make it. Individualism is the norm in countries such as the United States, Germany, and Australia, whereas collectivism is the norm in most of Asia, Africa, and Latin America (most of the world!). From an early age, collectivists are taught never to be the sore thumb that stands out because the sore thumb gets chopped off. Bringing honor to one's family and blending in with society is what is most highly valued.

When McDonald's began opening restaurants in India, a very collectivist culture, it soon learned it had to adapt its "employee of the month" program. Being singled out with rewards for excellent work is a strong motivator for many in individualist cultures, but it's a demotivating factor in a place where you're socialized to blend in. McDonald's wisely adapted its motivational program toward being the team or restaurant of the month. Understanding the primary source of identity—the individual or the group—is an insight that will shape whether you lead with cultural intelligence.

In individualist cultures, the pace of life is typically faster. Decisions happen expediently and that becomes expected of others. Little distinction is made between in-groups and out-groups. In collectivist cultures, loyalty to one's in-group, typically one's family and friends and sometimes one's colleagues, is of utmost importance. Social harmony is a top priority. It's been said that if Maslow had been Chinese, the top of his hierarchy of needs would have been social harmony rather than self-actualization.

The majority of the world is collectivist, but the majority of leadership literature is written by and for individualists. As more Asians, Latin Americans, and Africans publish their leadership perspectives, we will have more insights into leading in the collectivist context. In the meantime, we need to filter most of the leadership material we read with an eye toward how it needs to be adapted for the collectivists we encounter or lead. Understanding the implications of individualism versus collectivism is an essential part of growing your CQ Knowledge.[2]

Table 5-1. Individualism vs. Collectivism

Individualism		Collectivism	
Emphasis on individual goals and rights		Emphasis on group goals and personal relationships	
Individualist	*Moderate*	*Collectivist*	
Anglo Germanic Europe Nordic Europe	Eastern Europe Latin Europe	Arab Confucian Asia Latin America Southern Asia Sub-Saharan Africa	
For a description of the ten cultural clusters listed here, see Appendix 1. Note that most nations include people from multiple clusters (e.g., the dominant cluster in North America is Anglo and the dominant cluster in China is Confucian, but many other clusters exist in both places). The clusters simply provide a reference point for the largest cultural groups in the world.			
Leading Individualists • Motivate with personal incentives and goals. • Recognize that partnership usually involves one to two people, not a group.		**Leading Collectivists** • Motivate with group goals. • Recognize importance of long-term relationships.	

Power Distance

One morning when I was preparing to facilitate a leadership seminar in Delhi, I had an interesting interaction with my host, Sagar:

Dave: Are the training materials all printed and ready, Sagar?

Sagar: Oh, yes! They're at the print shop next door. They just need to be brought here.

Dave: Great! I'll run next door and get them.

Sagar: No, no. I'll send someone to get them.

Dave: That's kind of you, Sagar, but I don't mind at all. I can use the exercise after the long flight. It's no problem. I'll just run next door and come right back.

Sagar: Please wait here a while. We will drink tea and I'll have someone bring them to us.

Was Sagar just trying to be a gracious host? Should I have insisted on getting the materials or was I being too task oriented, missing that Sagar just wanted to have tea together? Or was he trying to save face and keep me from knowing they hadn't even been printed yet? Either of these could have been the reason Sagar was reluctant to let me get the materials. Interpreting the many possibilities behind this kind of exchange is something we'll explore further as we look at CQ Strategy. After I debriefed this experience with a couple of Indian colleagues and did some additional reading about norms in India, I began to see that this conflict over picking up a print order may have been primarily related to differing views between Sagar and me regarding power distance.

It seems I wasn't sufficiently status conscious to suit Sagar. A high power-distance culture views it as the lot of some individuals in life to courier materials and carry books while others are given the role of doing things such as teaching or being an executive. For me to have picked up my own things would have been a slight on Sagar, demonstrating he didn't know how to take care of a guest teacher. And it's possible it may have been a slur on the importance of education itself. By the way, the materials showed up right on time.[3]

Power distance refers to the amount of distance that is expected between leaders and followers. Countries scoring high in power distance—such as Mexico, India, and Ghana—offer a great deal of formal respect to leaders. Titles and status are revered, leaders and followers are unlikely to socialize together, and subordinates are not expected to question their superiors. Power distance is the extent to which differences in power and status are expected and accepted. It reveals where the power lies and how it's structured.

Again, this value varies not only in national cultures but also across other cultural contexts including generational subcultures, professional cultures, and organizational cultures. When visiting a new organization, notice how individuals address the people to whom they report, what kinds of titles are used, and how they're displayed. How are you introduced to the senior leader and what does the office setup suggest about power dynamics? Don't miss these important observations when you're in the interviewing process with a new organization or when you're courting a client in a new cultural context.

Individuals from high power-distance cultures who come to work in the United States often demonstrate their discomfort with the attitudes toward authority figures that differ from what they see at home. An engineer from India said, "The first time my North American supervisor told me, 'I don't know,' I was shocked. I asked myself, 'Why is he in charge?' In my country, a superior would give a wrong answer rather than admit ignorance."

An international student from Indonesia, another culture scoring very high in power distance, made this comment about her experience coming to study at a U.S. university:

> I was surprised and confused when on leaving Whittier Hall the provost . . . held the door for me. . . . I was so confused that I could not find the words to express my gratefulness, and I almost fell on my knees as I would certainly do back home. A man who is by far my superior is holding the door for me, a mere student and a nobody.[4]

Canada, Germany, Finland, Austria, and Israel are described as some of the lowest power-distance cultures in the world. In low power-distance cultures, most people feel at ease socializing with their leaders and addressing them as peers. Subordinates feel free to question their managers and they expect to have input in the decision-making process.[5]

Leading with cultural intelligence requires adapting your leadership style for various value orientations. I prefer a participative style of leadership (low power distance) in which status is downplayed and people's opinions are equally valued. I'm not a big fan of formal titles, and for me, the flatter the organizational chart the better. But as I come to understand the way my culture's low power distance shapes my leadership preferences, it's also helping me to see how high power distance shapes the preferred styles of leadership among others. Subordinates in high power-distance cultures expect leaders to tell them exactly what to do. At the very least, if I insist on using a more empowering, participative style of leadership in a place like India, I have to creatively figure out how to make that work and I need to accept that multiple leadership styles can be effective.

I experience the contrast in power distance when I move between the Middle East and Western Europe. But I also experience it between organizational cultures such as more top-down, authoritative structures within U.S. government agencies and the military as compared to when I interact with leaders from Facebook, a place described by insiders as anti-hierarchical and title agnostic. In fact, I recently interviewed Bill McLawhon, head of leadership development at Facebook, and I asked him how their low power distance culture shapes the way they work globally. I said to Bill:

> You've described a very strong culture at Facebook—hierarchy agnostic, fast, autonomous, no victims/excuses, take risks, etc. Many of these values are diametrically opposite to the core values of most developing world cultures. How is that influencing your approach to leadership development globally?

Bill responded:

> You're absolutely right and I know this can be an issue. We've already observed it among some of our teams. We want to find the right individuals globally who are culturally synchronous with both their local context and Facebook. It won't work if they can't bridge both cultures.
>
> We'll cease to be Facebook if we eliminate all our core values from how we operate. But we're conscious of this challenge and it's one of the things that we'll be prioritizing most this next year—how do we develop high performing teams who can effectively utilize our diversity across the world to make even greater impact?[6]

This is the kind of insight and intentionality we're seeking by learning about these cultural value dimensions. Leaders and organizations may decide not to adapt to some of the cultural norms of various places where they work, but before you can make that strategic decision—something we'll look at in the next chapter— we have to first understand that there are equally valid ways of approaching leadership and power distance. The best leadership approach depends on the organization, the followers involved, and the task to be accomplished.

Table 5-2. Power Distance

Low Power Distance		High Power Distance	
Emphasis on equality; shared decision making		Emphasis on differences in status; decisions made by superiors	
Low	*Moderate*		*High*
Anglo Germanic Europe Nordic Europe	Confucian Asia Eastern Europe* Latin Europe* Sub-Saharan Africa		Arab Latin America Southern Asia*
For a description of the ten cultural clusters listed here, see Appendix 1. *Indicates significant variation within cluster.			
Leading Low Power-Distance Individuals • Forgo formalities. • Create ways to question or challenge authority.		**Leading High Power-Distance Individuals** • Follow chain of command carefully. • Do not question or challenge authority.	

Uncertainty Avoidance

Uncertainty avoidance is the extent to which you are at ease with unknown, unpredictable outcomes. High uncertainty avoidance is a discomfort with ambiguity and uncertainty. People oriented toward high uncertainty avoidance focus on ways to reduce ambiguity, and they create structures to help ensure some measure of predictability. For example, someone leading staff primarily from the high uncertainty avoidance cultures in Germany, Japan, or Singapore would be wise to give very clear instructions and timetables for when and how the assignment should be completed. Simply telling an employee to write a plan in order to competently address the problem may create all kinds of dissonance for a team member oriented toward high uncertainty avoidance.

On the other hand, cultures scoring lower in uncertainty avoidance, such as Britain or Saudi Arabia, are not as threatened by unknown situations and what lies ahead. Open-ended instructions, varying ways of doing things, and loose deadlines are more typical in these kinds of cultures. These are places where ambiguity and unpredictability are welcomed. Strict laws and rules are resisted and people are more accepting of opinions different from theirs.[7]

Uncertainty avoidance is also a way to understand the differences that exist between two cultures that might otherwise seem to be much the same. For example, Germany and the United Kingdom have a great deal in common. Both are in Western Europe, both speak a Germanic language, both had relatively similar populations before the German reunification, and the British royal family is of German descent. Yet the person who understands the uncertainty avoidance dimension will quickly notice considerable differences between life in Frankfurt and life in London. Punctuality, structure, and order are modus operandi in German culture, whereas Brits are much more easygoing regarding time and deadlines and tend to be less concerned about precision than Germans. This can be explained in part by the different views the cultures have toward the unknown. But remember, as I've continually noted, we can't make blanket assumptions about everyone from a culture. Not all Brits and Germans will view uncertainty and risk in the same way. These cultural values are just one aspect of applying cultural intelligence. But they're a helpful place to begin anticipating how our leadership might unfold when encountering differing degrees of tolerance for ambiguity and the unknown.

I spend a lot of time in Singapore. Some studies have erroneously labeled Singapore as low uncertainty avoidance. That would mean Singaporeans, like Brits, are comfortable with ambiguity and open-ended conclusions. Although Singapore is cosmopolitan and allows for many value orientations, the dominant orientation in Singapore is to plan carefully and develop contingency plans.[8] It's not uncommon for me to be asked twelve to fifteen times in advance of speaking at an event in Singapore to provide an additional level of clarity about what I'll be covering. Even after I provide as clear an explanation as I know how, I'm often asked for further clarification. Similarly, when my wife and I lived there, Singaporean parents often cautioned us against allowing our kids to

Table 5-3. Uncertainty Avoidance

Low Uncertainty Avoidance		High Uncertainty Avoidance	
Emphasis on flexibility and adaptability		Emphasis on planning and predictability	
Low	*Moderate*		*High*
Anglo Eastern Europe Nordic Europe	Arab Confucian Asia* Germanic Europe Southern Asia* Sub-Saharan Africa		Latin America Latin Europe

For a description of the ten cultural clusters listed here, see Appendix 1.
*Indicates significant variation within cluster.

Leading Low Uncertainty Avoidance Individuals	**Leading High Uncertainty Avoidance Individuals**
• Avoid dogmatic statements. • Invite them to explore the unknown. • Let them act and keep you informed.	• Give explicit instructions. • Rely on formalized procedures and policies. • Ask them to recommend action; then offer feedback and support.

freely climb up and down the playground equipment in the park. It seemed the cultural aversion to risk caused them to be extremely cautious about the ways they would allow their children to play. Whether it is investing or exploring different faith traditions or teaching methodologies, traditionally the Singaporean culture is much more comfortable with boundaries and predictable certainty. Singaporeans often view their highly involved government with many laws as a small price to pay for safety and certainty. This doesn't mean that high uncertainty cultures avoid risk altogether. In fact, Singapore and Germany have often been leaders in pursuing innovative technologies and research. But for a high uncertainty avoidance culture, risk is carefully calculated and planned for, rather than taken as an inevitable part of life, as would be more likely in low uncertainty avoidance cultures.

Cooperative vs. Competitive

The next cultural orientation is called cooperative versus competitive. Cultures more oriented around the cooperative orientation emphasize nurturing, supportive relationships as a better way of getting things done. In contrast, individuals and cultures more oriented toward the competitive orientation are more focused on achievement, success, and competition to accomplish results. Both orientations are concerned about results but it's a matter of how best to accomplish them.

Another way to think about this cultural difference is to consider how you feel when you watch a political debate. Do you like to see your preferred candidate be confrontational, aggressive, and attack his or her opponent? Or do you have more respect for candidates who are conciliatory, collaborative, and deferential to one another? I'm assuming you want your candidate to have a backbone and conviction. But what's the overall tone and approach that will most earn your confidence and respect?

Some of the most cooperative-oriented cultures in the world are Thailand, Sweden, and Denmark. Their cooperative orientation can be seen in the way they approach business and international relationships. National interests, business results, and profits are valued, but they believe the best way to accomplish these things is through collaboration. Many Scandinavian companies look for managers who are adept at shaping business deals by putting together cooperative alliances and teams. In cooperative cultures, people are less likely to be praised individually for their accomplishments because cooperation with others is accepted as the most important goal. It's generally thought that in cooperative societies, noteworthy achievements and successes are less the result of one person's leadership or brilliance and more the result of a group of people working together.

In contrast, a competitive culture is focused on getting ahead. A child's report card from a school in a competitive culture might make brief reference to how the student behaves with others, but the primary emphasis is on the child's personal achievements in each subject area. The guiding principle for those who are more competitively oriented is "survival of the fittest." The tough are going to win the most, so you have to play that way. Competition will force you to innovate, adapt, and thrive; otherwise you'll become obsolete. Most of the Western business world is largely organized around the competitive orientation. In these contexts, a company pays little attention to an employee's personal life. Employees are expected to independently resolve any personal issues that might affect their work responsibilities. And although various managers might take an interest in their employees' personal lives, ultimately, the company's job in competitive cultures is to win. Jack Welch, former CEO of GE, is the epitome of the competitive orientation. He's well known for his ruthless emphasis on meeting targets and results, and he often said a company ideally would have every manufacturing plant on a barge so it can be moved to where the wages are lowest.[9]

A Chinese friend of mine from Hong Kong recently told me how confused he was by the behavior of a North American colleague who visited him in Hong Kong. My friend and his North American colleague had worked together for a few years, but all their communication had been virtual. When they finally met in Hong Kong, they worked hard together the first morning. My friend said it was a typical morning working with a Westerner—all very task focused and, frankly, similar to the dominant approach to work in Hong Kong. But then they went to lunch together. During lunch, the North American was extremely warm and relational and acted like he and my Chinese friend were very close. In fact, the North American began telling my friend about his messy divorce, including sultry details about his ex-wife's affair. My friend was extremely uncomfortable with the whole situation. He said to me, "I've had close friends who got divorced and I didn't learn about it for years. But here I was hearing this from a guy I only met this morning."

The most jarring moment came when the two men went back to the office after lunch. As soon as they returned, the North American shifted back fully into work mode and started writing up the proposal they had started discussing only that morning. He was insistent that each man's name be listed with the specific sections each one had developed so that credit would go where credit was due.

My Chinese friend has a cooperative orientation, and as a result, he sees things such as intimacy, competition, and taking personal credit as conflicting priorities. He expected a highly competitive task orientation from his North American colleague. But he was completely caught off guard by hearing personal, intimate details from him over their first meal together. In the future, my Chinese friend had a better understanding of the way many North Americans mix a personal, friendly approach with an otherwise

Table 5-4. Cooperative vs. Competitive

Cooperative		Competitive	
Emphasis on collaboration and nurturing behavior to get results		Emphasis on competition, assertiveness, and achievement to get results	
Cooperative	*Moderate*		*Competitive*
Nordic Europe Sub-Saharan Africa	Arab Confucian Asia Eastern Europe Latin America Latin Europe Southern Asia*		Anglo Germanic Europe

For a description of the ten cultural clusters listed here, see Appendix 1.
*Indicates significant variation within cluster.

Leading Cooperative Individuals	**Leading Competitive Individuals**
• Establish the relationship before completing the task. • Build trust on the basis of care for personnel and family.	• Complete the task before building the relationship. • Build trust on the basis of results.

task-oriented, transactional approach. As a result, he found himself better prepared for future interactions with this colleague and others because he had shifted his expectations.

Short Term vs. Long Term

There are a variety of ways to compare the way our cultures socialize us to think about time. One of the most helpful contrasts for leaders to understand is short-term versus long-term orientation, or what might be thought of as an emphasis on the *present* versus an emphasis on the *future.* This is the extent to which you're willing to wait for results and rewards.

Cultures that expect and demand results in the very near future are short-term-oriented cultures; those that are more focused on the long-term payoff are called long-term-oriented cultures. Once I was reading an article in a Singaporean newspaper that reported on new health care legislation that had just been approved. The initial implementation, the article said, would begin in about ten years. I imagined that if people in the United States, a very short-term-oriented culture, learned that the U.S. federal government had approved legislation that would begin rolling out in a decade, most of them would think that was ludicrous. But for Singapore, where there's a longer time orientation, such a time frame is acceptable.

U.S. political cycles are perhaps one of the clearest examples of short-term time orientation. Americans put a political party in office and expect its members to get to work. Results from their efforts are expected within the first few months. If they haven't made significant change in eighteen months, the party is voted out of office and the other one put in. And the cycle repeats itself. There is very little patience for long-term plans that don't provide some type of immediate solutions.

In a short-term orientation, people look at what has happened in the recent past and make decisions that will lead to quick results. Anglo cultures, which are found most in North America, the United Kingdom, and Australia, are some of the most short-term-oriented cultures in the world, but short-term priorities are also the norm in places such as the Philippines and throughout Sub-Saharan Africa. This is believed to stem from cultures having originated from a maritime civilization where seafaring societies were more open to taking risks for their immediate survival and benefit.[10] Businesses in short-term-oriented cultures look for quick wins that show up in quarterly results and annual returns. This certainly varies depending on the kind of industry a business is in, but shareholders typically expect timely returns.

The long-term orientation is most often associated with Confucian cultures, which includes Japan, Korea, and China. These cultures strongly value perseverance, a key aspect of the long-term time orientation, and "thrift" is highly valued. Long-term-oriented cultures have a higher savings rate among people and there are usually high national reserves. Compared to the seafaring societies in the West, Chinese culture originated from an insulated land civilization. Ancestry and tradition are held in high esteem, and

Table 5-5. Short Term vs. Long Term

Short Term		Long Term	
Emphasis on immediate outcomes (success now)		Emphasis on long-term outcomes (success later)	
Short Term	*Moderate*	*Long Term*	
Anglo Arab Eastern Europe Nordic Europe Sub-Saharan Africa	Germanic Europe Latin America Latin Europe Southern Asia	Confucian Asia	
For a description of the ten cultural clusters listed here, see Appendix 1.			
Leading Short-Term-Oriented Individuals		**Leading Long-Term-Oriented Individuals**	
• Help them get to "quick wins." • Focus on the present.		• Save now for the future. • Emphasize the long-term success—past and future.	

this, together with a value for order and harmony, means that short-lived ideas are viewed with greater caution.[11]

People who do international development work often feel challenged by the short-term versus long-term time orientation. Development workers are often addressing problems in places such as Haiti that cannot be quickly solved. They require a very long-term view. Yet these development leaders report that most of their donors are from short-term-oriented cultures and that they often stop giving when they don't see results in a short period of time. Both groups would benefit from understanding the assets and potential limitations of a short-term or long-term view.

Context: Direct vs. Indirect

The next cultural value explains one of the most prevalent forms of conflict that occurs on multicultural teams: direct versus indirect communication. Direct communicators are often frustrated by what they perceive as obtuse, unclear communication from their intercultural counterparts. And indirect communicators are offended by what sounds like a blunt, rude style from some Westerners.

Even teams that make the effort to create ground rules for team communication bump up against this cultural difference. A team leader recently told me she insists on respectful communication across any team she leads, regardless of the circumstances. But how you define "respectful communication" varies significantly based on your cultural background. A typical New Yorker or German leader will believe the most respectful way to interact with a team member is to say it like it is. Don't beat around the bush or sugarcoat things. Be direct. Anything else is disingenuous and may even be perceived as passive-aggressive or deceptive. However, a typical Mexican or Chinese leader will believe the most respectful way to interact with a team member is to save face, particularly in the midst of a conflict. The thinking goes something like this: *Why would I need to disrespect you by stating what's painfully obvious to both of us?* Retaining harmony and the relationship is the driving value.

This cultural value dimension is referred to as "context" because an indirect, high-context individual pays as much attention to the context, body language, and what's *not* said as to what *is* said, whereas a direct, low-context individual draws very little meaning from the context and just pays attention to the words spoken. For a low-context individual, you should "mean what you say and say what you mean" and not rely on implied meaning.

Personality and gender definitely influence the degree to which you value low-context (direct) versus high-context (indirect) communication. But culture also shapes this. An Israeli might perceive herself as indirect (Israel is one of the most direct cultures in the world), but may still seem rather direct to someone from a high-context culture (e.g., Japan). And a Japanese individual may view himself as very direct but may still seem indirect to someone coming from a direct culture (e.g., Israel). So there's relativity to how this cultural difference is experienced.

High-context cultures are places where people have significant history together and so a great deal of understanding can be assumed. Things operate in high-context cultures as if everyone there is an insider and knows how to behave. Written instructions and explicit directions are minimal because most people know what to do and how to think.

Our families are probably the most tangible examples we have of high-context environments. After years of being together, we know what the unspoken rules are of what to eat, how to celebrate holidays, and how to communicate with each other. Many of our workplaces are also high context. We know when to submit check requests, how to publicize an event, and what different jargon and acronyms mean. New employees joining these kinds of organizations can feel lost without adequate orientation. Similarly, many religious services are also very high context. People routinely stand, bow, or recite creeds that appear foreign and confusing to someone attending for the first time.

Low-context cultures are usually places where people have less history together. Most national cultures across Europe and North America are predominantly low context. Many of the connections among people and places are of a shorter duration, and therefore less is assumed. This emerges not only through interpersonal communication but also in viewing the kind of instructions that are displayed. Signs about where to park, how to flush the toilet, and where to order your food are more likely displayed in places where many outsiders visit. Extra attention is given to providing information about how to act. Low-context cultures are easier to enter than high-context cultures because even if you're an outsider much of the information needed to participate is explicit. But bear in mind how jarring it can be for a high-context visitor to be affronted with what may seem like rude, aggressive communication.

It's difficult for any multicultural team to function entirely in a high-context way. Even if all the team members come from a high-context orientation, different contexts presume different meanings (e.g., where you sit around a conference table may mean you're the leader in one context and an outside guest in another). Leaders of multicultural teams need to go beyond simply asking that communication be "respectful" and discuss how respect is manifested for the various participants. Very direct communicators may need to soften their blunt edge and very indirect communicators may need to work toward being more explicit to ensure the rest of the team understands.[12]

Table 5-6. Direct vs. Indirect Context

Low Context (Direct)		High Context (Indirect)	
Emphasis on explicit communication (words)		Emphasis on indirect communication (tone, context)	
Low	*Moderate*	*High*	
Anglo Germanic Europe Nordic Europe	Eastern Europe Latin America Latin Europe	Arab Confucian Asia Southern Asia* Sub-Saharan Africa	
For a description of the ten cultural clusters listed here, see Appendix 1. *Indicates significant variation within cluster.			
Leading Low-Context (Direct) Individuals		**Leading High-Context (Indirect) Individuals**	
• Email instructions and updates. • Be explicit: "Here's what I need. . . ." • Apologize when you make a mistake.		• Discuss instructions and updates. • Be indirect. "I wonder if. . . ." • Apologize when harmony is disrupted.	

Being vs. Doing

The story is often told of a New York businessman who is vacationing in a little coastal village in Mexico. Every morning, he sees a Mexican fisherman get in a boat, go out for an hour or two, and come back with a great catch of fish. One morning, the New Yorker starts talking with the man:

New Yorker: It looks like you gather a big catch of fish every day.

Fisherman: Oh, yes. There's no shortage out there. You could catch fish all day long.

New Yorker: Then why don't you stay out longer and catch more?

Fisherman: Well, this is more than enough to support my family's needs for today.

New Yorker: So what do you do with the rest of your day?

Fisherman: I fish a little, play with my kids, take an afternoon siesta, and then I stroll into the village each evening, where I have a beer and play guitar with my amigos. I have a full life.

New Yorker: I can help you. You should spend more time fishing, and with the proceeds, you could buy a bigger boat. Then you could catch even more fish, and with that income you could buy several boats. Eventually you would have a fleet of fishing boats. Instead of selling your catch to a middleman, you would sell directly to the processor. And eventually you could open your own cannery. You would control the product, the processing, and the worldwide distribution. You could leave this little coastal fishing village and move to Mexico City, then Los Angeles, and eventually New York, where you could run your ever-expanding enterprise.

Fisherman: (looking interested but perplexed): But, how long will all this take?

New Yorker: I don't know, fifteen to twenty years. But when the time is right, you can sell your company and become very rich. You would make millions.

Fisherman: Okay, but then what?

New Yorker: Then you could retire. You could move to a small coastal fishing village, where you could fish a little, play with your grandkids, take a siesta, and stroll into the village to have a beer and play your guitar with your amigos.

The Mexican walks away confused about why he would go to all that effort to regain the very life he already has.

The Mexican was operating from a "being" orientation to life, and the New Yorker was operating from a "doing" orientation. All cultures value time. But how we use our time is strongly influenced by our cultural background. Someone with a being orientation works and may work very hard, but he works to live, whereas someone with a doing orientation lives to work. The Mexican fisherman works so he can enjoy his life with his friends and family. Work probably plays a limited role in how he defines his identity. Upon meeting you for the first time, it probably wouldn't occur to him to talk to you right away about being a fisherman; instead, he would be more likely to tell you about his parents, his wife, his kids, and his friends. And it may not occur to being-oriented individuals that they should strive to work with passion and derive great significance from their work.

In contrast, the New York businessman is a picture of what it means to be shaped by the doing orientation. He's always thinking about how things can be turned into a more efficient, business-making opportunity. He likely asks, "So what do you do?" upon first meeting someone, and that will play a big part in how he figures out how he relates to that person. It's not that the businessman doesn't care about his family and friendships—he may very well take grand vacations to Mexico to relax and spend time with his family—but his psyche is largely oriented around his work and performance.[13]

If you're a doing-oriented leader, you might be tempted to view all being-oriented people as lazy. Or if you're a being-oriented leader, you might think all doing-oriented individuals can't relax. But neither is necessarily true. Instead, this is more about how someone is motivated: marking things off a to-do list or protecting a quality of life. Scandinavian cultures score high on the being orientation. A Swedish leader with low CQ might look at someone working sixty hours a week and think, "It's too bad he's so incompetent that he can't get the job done in thirty-five hours a week." But with higher CQ, the Swedish leader will understand it's just a different approach to getting work done and finding significance in life. A U.S. leader (likely high in doing) with low CQ might look at someone who leaves work early to pick up his kids as someone who isn't very committed to the job. But with higher CQ, that

Table 5-7. Being vs. Doing

Being	Doing	
Emphasis on quality of life	Emphasis on being busy and meeting goals	
Being	*Moderate*	*Doing*
Arab Latin America Nordic Europe Sub-Saharan Africa	Confucian Asia* Eastern Europe Latin Europe Southern Asia*	Anglo Germanic Europe
For a description of the ten cultural clusters listed here, see Appendix 1. *Indicates significant variation within cluster.		
Leading Being-Oriented Individuals	**Leading Doing-Oriented Individuals**	
• Create opportunities for personal growth. • Affirm who the person "is" first and foremost. • Manage the relationship.	• Provide training and development. • Affirm accomplishments. • Manage the process.	

leader will understand that hardworking individuals who use their time differently can still be efficient. Of course, there are plenty of people who are lazy and many who are workaholics. But that's not really the point here. Before you're too quick to judge someone's work ethic and personal life, consider how the individual's being versus doing orientation shapes how he or she functions. And when pitching an idea to someone, consider whether the person is being or doing oriented so you can make a compelling case.

Universalism vs. Particularism

The next cultural value dimension refers to the standard we use to judge people's behavior. Universalist cultures believe there are rules for everyone and no one gets to ignore them. This orientation emphasizes an obligation to adhere to standards that are universally agreed to by the societies in which we live. Because the universalist approach to life is rule based, behavior tends to be viewed in the abstract. For a universalist, your relationship with someone should have nothing to do with whether you apply the rules to that individual. If someone breaks a rule, that has to be addressed, regardless of who they are.

Particularist cultures believe we have special obligations to people we know. Particularist judgments focus on the exceptional nature of present circumstances. And you can't possibly treat every situation and person the same; it doesn't make sense. For a particularist, a friend who breaks a rule is not just an arbitrary person; he or she is a friend and has unique importance. So an individual from this orientation would sustain, protect, and defend a friend no matter what an arbitrary rule says.[14]

Andres Tapia, a former chief diversity officer at Hewitt Associates, grew up in Peru, a very particularist culture. Andres experienced great frustration when he first moved to the United States to study at Northwestern University. He had a problem paying his tuition every month. He received some financial aid, but his dad, who was in Peru, still had to pay a portion of the monthly bill. During this time, Peru was in utter turmoil. The country was being hit by terrorism and hyperinflation, and there were restrictions on transferring money out of the country—particularly to the United States. To get around the restrictions, Andres's dad had to send cash to people he trusted who were flying from Peru to the States. So the money always came to Andres, but it was usually a few weeks late.

Tuition for all Northwestern students was due on the fifteenth of every month, and if it was even a day late, a late fee was charged. On the fifteenth of most months, Andres would go to the bursar's office and say, "I'm sorry, but my money isn't in yet. I'll give it to you the second it arrives." The response was always the same: "There's a fifty-dollar fee for being late." Andres would explain, "But the money has been sent. It's coming from Peru. There's inflation, terrorism, and restriction on dollars. Can you please make an exception?" The university's response, from a universalist point of view, was always the same: "If we make an exception for *you*, we'd have to make an exception for everyone." Exasperated and coming from a particularist perspective, Andres one day said, "I'm sorry. How many students do you have who come from a country 6,000 kilometers away where there is a 15,000 percent cumulative hyperinflation rate, a growing terrorist movement igniting car bombs in the capital, and restrictions for getting dollars out of the country?" But his question changed nothing. He had to follow the rules established by the university.[15]

What's fair? Applying one rule equally to everyone or accounting for unusual circumstances? Most of us who have traveled have experienced the custom of haggling over the cost of an item. It can be kind of fun the first time you do it, but some travelers find it very frustrating. They just want to know what the price is. Many cultures, however, presume the price should vary based on the person buying it. If you visit the Taj Mahal in India, you will notice there's a very different cost for foreigners than there is for Indians. From a universalist perspective, this seems entirely unfair. Why should the cost change? But from a particularist perspective, it's extremely fair. Why would you charge the same amount to someone who has the money to travel from the other side of the world to see the beloved Taj Mahal as you would someone who may never make as much as the visitor's airfare in his or her entire lifetime? Universalists will be proponents of developing global standards that are

Table 5-8. Universalism vs. Particularism

Universalism		Particularism	
Emphasis on rules; standards that apply to everyone		Emphasis on specifics; unique standards based on relationships	
Universalist	*Moderate*	*Particularist*	
Anglo Germanic Europe Nordic Europe	Eastern Europe Latin Europe	Arab Confucian Asia* Latin America Southern Asia Sub-Saharan Africa	
For a description of the ten cultural clusters listed here, see Appendix 1. *Indicates significant variation within cluster.			
Leading Universalist Individuals • Provide commitments in writing and make every effort to abide by them. • When circumstances require a change, provide as much rationale and advance warning as possible.		**Leading Particularist Individuals** • Demonstrate flexibility whenever possible. • Invest in relationships and show the role of context in informing your decisions.	

followed consistently across an organization's global operations. Particularists will believe that standards and decisions need to be localized and personalized based on the specific context and relationships involved.

Neutral vs. Affective

In neutral-oriented cultures, people make a great effort to control how they express their emotions. People try not to reveal what they're thinking or how they're feeling. In affective cultures, people want to find ways to express their emotions, even spontaneously. In these cultures, it's welcomed and accepted to show your emotions.

One time I was working with a group of young Japanese executives and it was difficult to know whether they understood my presentation. As members of a very neutral culture, they offered virtually no nonverbal feedback. I observed a South African making a presentation to this same group of Japanese executives and I could tell she was also frustrated by the lack of responsiveness. So she began to ask questions of various individuals, such as: "What do you think about this, Yoshi-san?" She called them out by name but most of them still did not respond. In fact, most looked down and several of them quietly giggled. Giggling can often be an indicator in a neutral culture that people feel embarrassed and uncomfortable. They don't want to be put on the spot but they also don't want to express their discomfort, so the response is a nervous giggle. The presenter ended up forgoing her approach and asked for written feedback at the end of the presentation, something that seemed to give her far better input.

Neutral versus affective is not whether we feel emotions; it's the *way* we express emotions. In neutral cultures, such as the United Kingdom, Sweden, the Netherlands, Finland, Germany, and most Confucian Asian cultures, the dominant norm is to disguise what one is thinking or feeling and to limit the use of facial expressions and body language. Being cool and in control is admired, although sometimes this leads to unexpected outbursts, which become all the more jarring. Speaking is usually done in a more monotonic manner; it lacks an emotional tone and it's preferred that you "stick to the point" rather than go off on numerous tangents. In many neutral cultures—particularly throughout Asia—silence is not only okay, it's welcomed. Silence is a sign of respect and it allows both parties to reflect and take in what has been said.

In affective-oriented cultures such as Italy, Poland, and France, or among African Americans in the United States, the norm for communicating is a wider range of facial expressions and physical gestures. Individuals who don't show much expression may be viewed as cold or perhaps as lacking the confidence to express themselves. People with an affective orientation talk loudly when they're excited, and they love the art of arguing and debate. They're more enthusiastic and spontaneous and they consider their emotions and intuitions in their decision-making process. Statements are often emotional and dramatic and may often be exaggerated simply to make a point. Sometimes individuals in these cultures have learned that the only way you'll be heard is if you interrupt and raise your voice.[16]

This value difference can be seen across different socioeconomic groups as well. The United States as a whole falls moderately between neutral and affective. A typical American might roll her eyes at someone who flies off the handle too quickly, yet there is an expectation for people to express warmth, enthusiasm, and responsiveness as they interact with people or learn new information. But the working class in the United States has traditionally been more affective, with families and workplaces finding it normal to shout to someone or let out a boisterous laugh. In contrast, the dominant norm among professional middle- and upper-middle-class subcultures is a more controlled, nuanced way of expressing

Table 5-9. Neutral vs. Affective

Neutral		Affective	
Emphasis on non-emotional communication; hiding feelings		Emphasis on expressive communication; sharing feelings openly	
Neutral	*Moderate*		*Affective*
Confucian Asia Eastern Europe Germanic Europe Nordic Europe	Anglo* Southern Asia		Arab Latin America Latin Europe Sub-Saharan Africa

For a description of the ten cultural clusters listed here, see Appendix 1.
*Indicates significant variation within cluster.

Leading Neutral Individuals	Leading Affective Individuals
• Manage your emotions and regulate your body language. • Stick to the point in meetings and interactions.	• Open up to people to demonstrate warmth and trust. • Work on being more expressive than you might typically prefer.

emotions. Before being too quick to judge someone's behavior, consider how that person's orientation may be influencing what you observe.

Monochronic vs. Polychronic

The final cultural dimension we're going to cover comes back to the issue of time. Previously we reviewed the short-term versus long-term orientation toward time. But there's perhaps no cultural difference with which people more readily identify than whether or not 9 a.m. means 9 a.m. or something different. Although there are a few strategies we can use to deal with the different time orientations we encounter, one thing is clear: We're not going to change an individual's time orientation, much less an entire culture's. This is deeply cemented in the way people and societies function. But having some understanding of why people have such different orientations toward time can help reduce the conflict that occurs and provide a way for leading with cultural intelligence when different time orientations are involved.

Anthropologist Edward Hall describes the different time orientations of various cultures as monochronic and polychronic. Monochronic cultures use a linear approach to time. Schedules are moved through methodically, with things being checked off to-do lists and moving toward an identified goal. As a result, monochronic cultures value careful planning and place a great deal of attention on effective time management. And, typically, monochronic cultures value punctuality. The idea behind the term *monochronic* is that you focus on one task at a time. Most Western cultures are monochronic with the exception of some of the Latin European cultures. In an age when so many Westerners thrive on multitasking, it might seem counterintuitive to describe these cultures as monochronic. Many of us as leaders have to spin several plates at the same time. But this refers more to sequentially accomplishing tasks in a chronological order than whether you have multiple projects going on at the same time. In monochronic cultures, a high value is placed on intensely focusing on one thing at a time and carrying it through to completion. Leaders in monochronic cultures are taught to move through tasks in a linear fashion and may perceive those in polychronic cultures as being all over the place, not focused, and impossible to pin down.

The monochronic orientation also emphasizes the separation of personal life and work life. However, this is something that's become more difficult for any culture to pull off, given the proliferation of smartphones, constant email connectivity, and online social networking, and has become a source of great anxiety for many leaders. But in the monochronic context, there's a social protocol for when you should and shouldn't be connected to your phone. And if you've made a commitment to be at a 9 a.m. work meeting, to be late because you were helping your kids get off to school isn't a very viable excuse unless there were extenuating circumstances you couldn't have possibly planned for.

In contrast, Edward Hall describes the other end of the dimension as a polychronic time orientation. Polychronic societies are places where people's personal lives and work lives are much more intertwined. The emphasis for the polychronic-oriented individual is on fulfilling multiple responsibilities at one time. To the monochronic leader, this looks like a person who is easily distracted because that person will drop whatever he is doing to attend to anyone who calls or stops by. People in these cultures thrived on multitasking long before the age of smartphones and virtual work environments, but multitasking isn't driven by efficiency. It's a matter of reacting to things as they come along and weighing priorities in light of various roles and relationships.[17]

I often facilitate seminars with executives from a variety of places around the globe. The participants from monochronic cultures are usually present in the classroom all throughout the session. There may be a few who are consistently late or who seem to be focused on their phones, but the unspoken expectation among most of these leaders is that being out of the room or on one's phone is rude. If a monochronic participant does need to take a phone call, often the person apologizes to me for the disturbance. But executives from polychronic cultures, such as many Middle Eastern leaders, are much more apt to arrive at various times; come and go from the session; and receive whatever phone calls might come through or, at the very least, see very little need to disguise reading and responding to messages. It might make little sense to them to "switch off" their family or other work responsibilities during the session. In polychronic cultures, human interaction is valued over time and material things. As a result, there's less concern about and priority for "getting things done" efficiently and on time. Things will get done, but it will happen in due time. In the polychronic world, an individual's day is driven by one relationship and conversation to the next. The most extreme examples of polychronic cultures are the Aboriginal people and the Native American cultures. Tribal gatherings and "talking stick meetings"

Table 5-10. Monochronic vs. Polychronic

Monochronic		Polychronic	
Emphasis on a linear approach to time; work and personal lives kept separate		Emphasis on multitasking; can combine work and personal lives	
Monochronic	*Moderate*		*Polychronic*
Anglo Germanic Europe Nordic Europe	Confucian Asia* Eastern Europe Southern Asia		Arab Latin America Latin Europe* Sub-Saharan Africa
For a description of the ten cultural clusters listed here, see Appendix 1. *Indicates significant variation within cluster.			
Leading Monochronic Individuals • Provide follow-through and expediency when possible to build trust. • When a deadline can't be met, propose an alternative one and stick to it.		**Leading Polychronic Individuals** • Find ways to be flexible on deadlines that are less important. • Communicate the relational impact for you if a deadline isn't met.	

take place whenever they're needed, and they go on for as long as somebody has something to say. There's no need to rush it to conclusion, and doing so is considered rude and bad luck.

Conclusion

Leaders who live by the mantra "People are people and business is business" are unable to effectively lead collaborative work that involves people from diverse cultures. The failure of a leader to understand the profound differences in how cultural value orientations influence the way people are motivated, offer input, and go about their work will lead to global ineffectiveness. In contrast, leaders who grow in understanding the kinds of cultural differences we've reviewed in this chapter and Chapter 4 are better able to lead in a way that is both effective and respectful. And while I've primarily applied these value orientations by comparing one national culture with another, they can be equally useful in comparing different ethnicities, regional cultures, organizational cultures, etc.[18]

How do you effectively use the understanding gained by growing your CQ Knowledge without using it to stereotype people? And given the tendency with which people so quickly stereotype, why even use the kinds of generalizations we've examined in these two chapters? There's value in something that cross-cultural psychologists Joyce Osland and Allan Bird describe as "sophisticated stereotypes"—broad comparative differences based on empirical, intercultural research. Sophisticated stereotypes, such as those that stem from understanding the six cultural systems or the ten cultural dimensions, are most helpful when they are:

- Used to compare various cultures rather than to understand the behavior of a singular culture
- Consciously held

- Descriptive, not evaluative
- Used as a best first guess prior to having direct information about specific people
- Modified based on further observations and experience[19]

CQ Knowledge is not enough to lead with cultural intelligence. But it's a crucial step in being able to make sense of people and situations you need to manage. Of the four CQ capabilities, improving CQ Knowledge is the most straightforward. It simply involves taking the time to learn more about cultural differences. We can all grow in the extent to which we understand culture. The starting point for CQ Knowledge is understanding how culture shapes our own thinking and behavior. From there, we can draw on our self-awareness to learn about the influence of culture on others.

CQ KNOWLEDGE PRACTICES

1. *Study a foreign language.* You probably won't need to look far to find a teacher. Native speakers are usually the best teachers. Even learning a few phrases goes a long way when we travel abroad.

2. *Read international novels and memoirs.* Books like this one provide a conceptual framework for thinking about culture, but there's something far more visceral about reading novels like *The Kite Runner* or *White Man's Grave* or watching movies like *Gran Torino* or *Lost in Translation* to build CQ Knowledge. Enter another world through novels, memoirs, and movies set in another place.

3. *Be globally informed.* Tap into various news sources to get beyond the latest gossip about Hollywood celebrities. BBC News is one of the finest sources, along with public broadcasting. And try visiting Al Jazeera's website to see how the "same" events are described in very different ways. When traveling, pick up something other than your preferred international newspaper to get a local perspective.

4. *Gain some basic insights about where you're going.* Look up the "country profiles" on BBC's website. There's one for every country in the world. These provide you with a basic overview of a country, its history, and the key issues facing its people so that at least there's a place to begin conversations while there. Or review the extensive information available on global business for various regions and countries at http://globaledge.msu.edu.

5. *Go to the grocery store.* The products and layout of a grocery store in culturally different communities can be a fascinating way to observe cultural differences. Beware of making assumptions based on what you see, but do observe what's the same as and what's different from where you shop.

CHAPTER 6

CQ STRATEGY: DON'T TRUST YOUR C

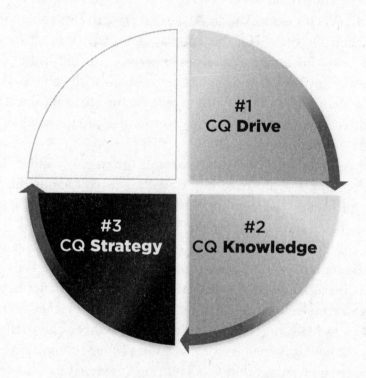

CQ STRATEGY: How should I plan?	
Strategizing and making sense of culturally diverse experiences	
Profile of a leader with high CQ Strategy	Leaders with high CQ Strategy develop ways to use their cultural understanding to develop plans for new intercultural situations. These leaders are better able to monitor, analyze, and adjust their assumptions and behaviors in different cultural settings. They are conscious of what they need to know about an unfamiliar culture.

135

My attempt to find out whether Dr. Jones in Liberia was a crook (as described in Chapter 1) was rooted in my North American orientation toward direct and explicit communication. I have little tolerance for dodging the elephant in the room, and though I surely value diplomacy, I prefer to address conflict directly and swiftly. When I arrived at the Monrovia airport, I was able to step back and see that Tim, the Liberian American visiting for two weeks, and his porter were not connecting. I could listen to the stories of my breakfast companions' mishaps with baby food and medical shipments. But I failed to take the time to think about how my direct, "name the elephant in the room" approach would shape my own success in Liberia.

If you had asked me about some of the values found in Liberian culture, I could have quickly talked to you about the high level of loyalty and commitment given to relationships. I think I even could have described the value of saving face for a friend and colleague above the value of providing accurate, shameful information to a stranger from another country. But I failed to use my cultural knowledge to effectively accomplish what I needed: a clearer understanding of whether we should partner with Dr. Jones and Madison College. Only as I stepped back and reflected on what had happened, as well as Moses's commentary, did I begin to better understand that I was putting Dr. Harris in what felt to him like an impossible situation. He comes from a cultural orientation that places less value on being straightforward and crystal clear than on keeping the honor of others intact while delivering the message. This conversation could have been more helpful if I had spent more time planning how to approach Dr. Harris with a contentious issue—something addressed by the third capability of cultural intelligence, CQ Strategy.

The next day, Moses and I were with another Liberian who used to teach at Madison College and, consequently, he also knew Dr. Jones, the alleged embezzler. Having spent some time thinking through the previous day's interactions, this time I used a very different approach. I began by asking what this Liberian leader perceived as some of the strengths of Dr. Jones and his school. At one point during the meeting, Moses, my host, excused himself to take a phone call, so I used the opportunity to ask the leader with whom we were meeting, "What might a school like ours find challenging in partnering with Dr. Jones's school?" I couched the question so he could offer feedback that wouldn't have to be considered a negative assessment of Dr. Jones and his school. The leader offered several points of caution, many of which closely aligned with the kinds of criticisms Moses had been offering. His critique was still indirect but the message between the lines was clear.

CQ Strategy is how we use the understanding we gain from CQ Knowledge. It helps us go beyond the surface and dive into the subtle but powerful issues that often make or break our leadership. As a result, CQ Strategy is the key link between our cultural understanding and behaving in ways that result in effective leadership.

One way to understand CQ Strategy is to think about the different ways we approach driving in various places. When I drive in places familiar to me, I'm prone to multitasking. If possible, I turn on the cruise control, listen to the radio, and often use the time to catch up on phone calls or talk with my passengers. But when I drive into a new city and need to find a destination, I slow down, turn off the radio, and minimize my conversation. Driving in a new place requires much more attentiveness. This is especially true if I'm in an area where motorists drive on the other side of the road. I feel more confident driving in new locations when I've planned ahead and looked at the directions for where I'm going. Sometimes the GPS directions don't account for unexpected construction. So even when I plan ahead, I have to remain alert to see whether I'm moving toward my destination. This is what CQ Strategy does for leading across cultures. It requires turning off the cruise control to become more conscious and alert about our surroundings;

this in turn allows us to develop an appropriate strategy for a new cultural situation. The three subdimensions measured in assessing a leader's CQ Strategy are planning, awareness, and checking.[1] These subdimensions offer important ways for applying the third capability of cultural intelligence: CQ Strategy.

HOW TO DEVELOP CQ STRATEGY

1. Plan cross-cultural interactions.
2. Become more aware.
3. Check whether your assumptions and plans were appropriate.

Key question: What do I need to plan to do this cross-cultural assignment successfully?

Plan Cross–Cultural Interactions

The first part of CQ Strategy is using our cultural understanding (CQ Knowledge) to plan for an interaction or project taking place in a different cultural environment. Most of us do a number of leadership tasks on autopilot. Pitching an idea to a client, addressing conflict on your team, or conducting a performance review are things that many of us have done numerous times as leaders. With experience, most leaders can do these tasks effectively without a whole lot of planning. However, when the cultural dynamics change, we'd be wise to spend time thinking about how we may need to alter our approach as compared to our default strategy. It's surprising how often leaders spend thousands of dollars to travel twenty-four hours to the other side of the world without having spent any time planning how to make the most of their time there.

I remember how amazed I was when I first learned that many introverts prepare for a cocktail party by planning possible conversations ahead of time. Anticipating who will be there, questions to ask, and remembering various details of people's lives is a coping strategy used by many introverts before heading to a social engagement. All personality types would be well served by using this kind of approach cross-culturally.

If you know you're going to be interacting cross-culturally, spend some time thinking about what and how you should communicate. This can be as simple as spending three minutes before a one-on-one meeting to consider the most effective approach. Ask yourself:

- What kind of small talk, if any, is appropriate for a person from this culture and for this individual?
- Who should initiate the transition from small talk into business?
- How will I get to action steps in this meeting?
- How much direction should I provide?

It's difficult to answer these questions without a growing measure of cultural understanding. Good CQ Strategy requires enhanced CQ Knowledge. By referring to the material covered in the previous two chapters, you'll at least have a decent hypothetical plan. Your cultural understanding serves as your GPS for navigating new terrain.

The first few times I had to drive on the left side of the road, unfamiliar territory for me, I had to remain very alert. But now that I've done it numerous times, even if I'm driving in a place new to me, it's easier than it was in the beginning. I've developed a few basic strategies for keeping track of what side I'm supposed to be on. Each new place brings with it new rules and challenges to my driving, but the more I drive in different places, the more adept I become at using heightened awareness to get to my destination. Ironically, the strategies I use in foreign places sometimes begin to change the ways I go about driving back home too. I find the same thing when leading across cultures.

Some of us have spent enough time leading cross-culturally that even the adaptations we make have become something we can do on autopilot. If that's the case, stop to consider how others on your team might *not* have the same level of experience and intuitive insight. Things as simple as avoiding the use of words such as *fall* and *spring* when communicating with someone from a different hemisphere or adjusting the level of formality used in writing an email (e.g., "Dear Dr. Wang" versus "Hi, Anne") are the subtle but powerful cues that demonstrate whether someone leads with cultural intelligence or not.

The real goal of CQ Strategy is to reflect on the lessons learned from one situation and accurately apply your insights to future situations. I will probably always experience disorienting and confusing encounters like the one I had in Liberia with Dr. Harris and Moses. But CQ Strategy and planning reduces the frequency and helps me learn from these situations so that I can better negotiate and lead in future interactions.

A leader with high CQ Strategy will actively create new strategies or adapt existing ones to deal with the new and unique aspects of an environment. This kind of leader is able to incorporate various observations and interpretations to create new strategies for new situations.[2] Most contexts provide ambiguous and often misleading cues about what is happening in an unfamiliar environment. We see familiar behaviors but the meaning is different. With planning, we've already primed ourselves to be more conscientious about whether a behavior means what it seems to mean. And that leads us to the next essential dimension of leading strategically across borders: awareness.

Become More Aware

The ability to be aware—of one's self, others, and a situation—is what really makes the difference between those who lead with cultural intelligence and those who don't. And the higher you go in the leadership ranks, the more difficult it becomes to be aware. Many CEOs are surrounded by people who laugh at their jokes, praise their ideas, and bite their tongues, even when they think an idea is stupid. It requires a very conscious effort to be a leader who remains aware and in touch with what's truly going on.

Plans and strategies can be dangerous if not coupled with awareness. Have you ever expected a leader from a particular organization or ethnicity to behave one way only to find out he was not at all like you anticipated? The goal is to hold our hypothetical plans very loosely and become aware of what's going on in the midst of the interaction to see whether the plan is appropriate. This requires slowing down long enough to become consciously aware of what's going on internally and externally as we lead in a multicultural world. Awareness is *stepping back from what we're doing and reflecting on it*. It's disciplining ourselves to see what we otherwise miss. Awareness is one of the primary tools that enables us to discern between the three levels of the iceberg (see Figure 4-1): What's universal, cultural, and personal? Awareness results in better decision making and overall performance.

Managing across cultures is rarely as simple as figuring out how a German and an Indian are going to interact. It's how *this* German woman from BMW is going to interact with *this* Indian man from Tata and vice versa. Some of the behavior may be typical of what you would expect from their respective cultures, but other aspects may just as easily be a reflection of the individual personalities and the situation at hand. By becoming aware, you can begin to discern whether the behavior you observe is typical for these individuals or whether they're actually adapting to you based on how they presume you want them to behave. Cultural adaptation doesn't just go in one direction, nor should it. The time you devote to becoming a more mindful leader will directly correlate with your development as a culturally intelligent leader, particularly in this area of awareness and leading strategically across cultures.

Becoming aware is an active process of drawing on the plans we develop using our CQ Knowledge and tuning into whether those plans suit particular situations. It's shutting down our semiautomatic impulses, suspending our assumptions for a period of time, and remaining aware throughout our cross-cultural experiences.

Look at the picture in Figure 6-1. What do you see? Take a moment to come up with an explanation for what's going on in this photo.

Figure 6-1. What Do You See?

This can be a fun exercise to do with your team. Ask them to view the photo and describe what's happening. You'll quickly see how strongly people believe in their interpretation of why the car is parked like it is. Many people who look at this picture will be confident that the car was parked by an inconsiderate, entitled executive who either didn't pay attention to the lines or thought he deserved multiple spaces. Others might suggest it was parked by a hurried parent who didn't have time to park within the lines or needed extra space to get a child out of the car because it is a two-door model. And some who live in snowy climates might think the car was parked this way because the parking lot was snow covered at the time and the person couldn't see the lines. The question is, *To what extent are you certain your explanation of the picture is accurate?* Without more information, we don't really know the story behind this picture. But our brain immediately rushes to interpret what's going on. And a great deal of interpretations stem from our own experiences and assumptions.

As leaders, we're often forced to read a situation quickly and interpret what's happening. It's risky doing that anytime, but it's particularly risky when different cultures are involved. For example, leaders who aren't used to someone sitting "silently" during a conversation may erroneously interpret that behavior as confusion or boredom. On the other hand, leaders from a culture where silence is often used as a form of respect may erroneously conclude someone is simply being respectful when, in fact, the person might be sending a message that she is bored or confused.

Awareness prepares us for the kinds of adaptations needed in most cross-cultural settings. When I walk into an organization's office for the first time, I observe what's on the wall, the office set-up, the way employees are dressed, and the titles used for various positions. Who gets invited to the meeting to discuss our proposal? Who holds the power? Who are the ultimate decision makers for this project? What are the vested interests behind the parties sitting at the table?

CQ Strategy is the way we answer the *why* questions behind what we experience and observe. *Why* does negotiation seem to consistently involve these dynamics here? *Why* is the leadership of this organization structured this way? *Why* is the office decorated like this?

When we're in a familiar environment, this process occurs with little effort. We know how to greet a business colleague as compared to a close friend. We can sell something on the fly or express empathy to a subordinate without much conscious effort. If we have some level of emotional intelligence, we know how to approach conflict and how to communicate in a familiar context. But with heightened awareness, we realize all these things might need to be done differently in a new cultural context. The sarcastic humor that seems to enhance informality and collegiality in one organizational culture might erode trust in another. Turning down a dinner invitation could be a deal breaker in one cultural context and inconsequential in another.

Self-Awareness

In Chapter 3, we considered the importance of being honest with ourselves about our interest in cross-cultural work (CQ Drive). A similar kind of honest introspection is important for developing CQ Strategy. Because organizations have better understood the importance of self-awareness for effective leadership, many human resources departments offer a variety of tools and assessments for becoming more personally aware as a leader. The discoveries we make through resources like these can help us grow in CQ Strategy. For example, my top strength on Gallup's StrengthsFinder is "Achiever," a characteristic of one who finds great satisfaction in hard work and productivity.[3] It's helpful for me to bear this in mind when I'm working in more laid-back cultures where relationships take priority over tasks. Through awareness, I have a better understanding of the personal frustration that often ensues when I feel like I haven't had a very productive day. I can also temper some of my frustration by redefining *productivity* in relational terms when working in more relationally driven cultures. With a heightened sense of awareness, we transcend merely being defined by our irritation or frustration and seek to understand what's behind it.

The degree to which we're self-aware partially stems from our understanding of own cultural contexts. And as we become aware of how our own behavior is shaped by culture, and of how others are likely to perceive us given our cultural background, we can begin to consciously accommodate for those perceptions. For example, it's one thing to understand that war and *Baywatch* are two predominant images many people around the world associate with Americans. But with awareness, U.S. leaders can look for cues as to whether the non-American with whom they're interacting has that perception.

Self-awareness offers us greater control over the many hours and dollars we invest in working with affiliates around the world. Burnout and fatigue are among the top negative consequences leaders associate with the growing demand to work across myriad cultures and time zones. Self-awareness is a key strategy for fending off a great deal of the frustration, burnout, and fatigue that occur in cross-cultural work.

Other-Awareness

As we gain an understanding of what's going on internally, we need to apply that same kind of awareness and understanding to others and to the environment around us. In my research on the experiences of North Americans who volunteer overseas for short periods of time, I have found that one of the critical gaps is an absence of awareness. Most of these volunteers travel to developing countries where they help with disaster relief, build medical clinics, teach English, or engage in religious mission work. Of all the comments made by these travelers on their return, the most common statement is something like, "Even though those people have so little, *they're so happy!*" There's something endearing about hearing a group of North Americans express their amazement that people with so little can be so content. My question is, Are the people they observed really happy? I've asked several hundred of these volunteers, "What makes you think they're happy?" They most often respond, "They were always smiling and laughing. And they were so generous to us. They fed us better than they themselves eat." Having observed these interactions firsthand myself, I agree that the locals typically greet foreign guests with big, warm smiles. But what do these behaviors really mean?

First, if you don't speak the language and you're just meeting someone for the first time, what do you do? After a few feeble attempts at saying things like "Hola!" or "Ni hau!" there's often laughter in response. It's really awkward. The locals in our example might be expressing happiness or their smiles and laughter might simply be a nervous response. This behavior in many cultures is as much an expression of embarrassment and nervousness as it is joy and happiness.

Then add that in places like Thailand there are twenty-three different smiles, each of which communicates something different. And in one small, extremely polite community in New Zealand, smiling is a way that people express their feelings that they have been deeply offended.[4] As I've continually said, the point isn't to learn every possible meaning of a behavior. But with heightened awareness of others, an individual will realize that although smiles might reflect genuine happiness, they just as well might be a nervous response that indicates little about the other person's level of contentment.

Awareness informed by CQ Knowledge will help us make more accurate interpretations. When anthropologists go into a civilization for the first time, their guiding mantra is "Hmm. I wonder why that is?" This is an excellent approach for us when observing the behavior of our team members and clients from different cultural backgrounds. Rather than too quickly assuming you know why someone always follows up a conference call with a lengthy email, ask yourself, *Hmm. I wonder why that is?* When you experience people in one particular region consistently arguing with you about any new initiative, again, use this mantra to guide your thinking on why this is happening. Eventually, you have to interpret the behavior and make a decision. But slow down how quickly you do so when cultural differences are involved.

Here are some other ways to become more aware of a diverse workforce and customer base:

- Spend at least 50 percent of the time you have with your direct reports *listening*. This is good advice anytime but particularly with staff who come from a different cultural background than you.
- Make regular appointments with your global partners just to hear their insights.
- Ask sales associates in various places what's selling (and what's not). Don't miss out on their frontline observations.
- Seek varied sources of input. Check online sources and see what people are watching from various parts of the world.
- Check out a variety of newspapers. What are the bestselling books and movies in London? In Dubai? In Moscow?
- Keep your eyes peeled for new trends in art, film, and theater.
- Look for unfamiliar behaviors (e.g., receiving your change with two hands) and see if it's consistently done by others. Ask a cultural coach if this is a norm.

These practices can serve us well in our own environment too, but they're particularly valuable for becoming more aware in different contexts. Awareness isn't something that needs to take a great deal of time. It's a strategy we can learn to use on the fly as we move in and out of various meetings, trips, and conversations. The simple discipline of seeing what we might otherwise miss is one of the best ways to develop CQ Strategy.

Check Whether Your Assumptions and Plans Were Appropriate

One more important way to develop CQ Strategy is to seek out information so you can determine whether your plans fit with what you are observing as you interact with people in other cultures. One time when I was doing some work in Manila, I arranged a dinner meeting with a Filipino man who had been asking for help in putting on a global leadership conference. Given my understanding of Filipino culture, I planned to make our meeting primarily social so that we could get to know each other. Based on how things went during dinner, I'd decide whether to talk about the conference near the end of dinner and formalize some next steps.

No sooner had we sat down at dinner than my Filipino counterpart asked me, "So what is this going to cost me?" I was a bit taken off guard. I wouldn't even expect such an abrupt, direct question from most Westerners. I wasn't sure whether this was my Filipino counterpart's typical way of interacting or if he was simply adapting to how he perceived a North American would want to interact. I wanted to test this a bit further so I responded, "Dinner is on me tonight. Please order whatever you like." He immediately replied, "I don't mean dinner. I mean if we bring you in to speak at this conference and if your center helps us with the planning and promotion." I decided to check one more time whether this was truly his preferred way of doing business, so I said, "We can certainly talk about that. But my goal tonight was to finally meet in person so we can get to know each other. And then we can figure out if and how to make this conference work." Then he retorted, "Well, it's wonderful to finally meet you, but if I don't have an idea of what kind of finances are involved, there's really no sense in discussing this any further."

I had developed my culturally intelligent plan based on my understanding of Filipino culture: Build relationships and allow the business transaction to flow from that. When I began to receive cues that my Filipino guest wanted a different approach, I checked my interpretation a couple more times. But by this point, it was clear that the Filipino norms didn't apply to this guy, at least not in this situation. I changed direction and we got down to business. Six months later I was honored to speak at a phenomenal conference he put together.

Checking, the final dimension of CQ Strategy, is looping back to reconsider whether the plan we have developed for a particular situation works. I often talk with midlevel Asian leaders working for Western multinational companies who perceive they can't break through the glass ceiling into upper levels of management. The reason they often cite is that they are perceived as lacking the confidence needed to be in senior leadership. Most of the Asian leaders who do break through have developed a plan for how to speak up more than they might typically do, given the value that many Western executives place on individual initiative for those promoted into senior leadership positions. On the other side, Western leaders need to be aware of when and how to speak up during meetings with Asians. Those with high CQ Strategy will observe the interactions and communication style of their Asian counterparts, such as turn taking, and will plan how and what to say before speaking up. Once they do so, they will work hard to monitor how their input is being received.[5] Whatever direction you adjust, when you gain the ability and confidence to function at this high level of cognitive processing, it's highly rewarding and results in some of the best intercultural practice. The three-part process of being aware, planning, and checking often happens almost simultaneously. The goal is to get more and more adept at planning ahead of time and remaining aware of what's going on in yourself and others as you interact, and to monitor whether your strategy is working.

In this process, it's really important for us to expect to misunderstand some things that happen as well as remain confused about others. At the very least, even a leader with extremely high CQ will encounter specific events and behaviors in a new cultural context that will not be immediately understood. In such cases, the leader delays judgment by suspending assumptions and sits with the uncomfortable state of not knowing. CQ Strategy includes accepting confusion and maintaining a willingness to not know something, which will lead to a better evaluation of the situation. That, in turn, will lead to eventual, and more accurate, understanding.[6] When we have that kind of understanding and strategy, we're poised for a level of culturally intelligent behavior that offers a competitive edge beyond what typically happens in the management of culturally diverse leaders—simply doing "business as usual" and leading from the gut. Though my way of getting information about Dr. Jones in Liberia was flawed, the input from my colleague Moses, combined with the intentional time I spent reflecting on the interaction and planning an alternative strategy, moved me beyond my initial impasse. My subsequent conversation was more planned and simultaneously monitored how the Liberian leader I was questioning responded to my approach and questions. In many regards, it made the difference between my trip being a waste of time and actually accomplishing one of my primary objectives.

Given the vast number of intercultural encounters experienced by most of us, it's unrealistic to know precisely what's going on at the deepest level of the iceberg for most of the individuals we encounter. That's a difficult process even with our intimate others. As the only male in my house, I regularly misunderstand what's going on around me with my own family. But at the very least, putting out our antenna to monitor the appropriateness of our assumptions and plan will enhance our cross-cultural leadership. Checking helps us confirm or disconfirm whether our interpretations are true and whether our subsequent plans are effective and strategic.

Conclusion

We ended up not partnering with Dr. Jones and Madison College in Monrovia, and I recently heard that Dr. Harris resigned from his teaching role at the college. I am, however, still using insights I learned from that situation. I'm currently in the midst of developing a strategic partnership with a few different organizations across China. We've received conflicting counsel about a particular Chinese leader and his business. Some advisers say we can't move forward in this region without this leader's involvement. Others caution us against any kind of partnership with him. Doing this kind of due diligence never becomes easy, but CQ Strategy is assisting me in developing a plan for how to get the information we need. China and Liberia are vastly different places. But some of the strategies I learned from my work in Liberia can be adapted for this current challenge in China.

Once you learn the skills for CQ Strategy, you can apply them to all kinds of relationships and situations. You can even look at a Goth teenager and ask yourself, *What's behind the black clothes, piercings, tattoos, and music?* rather than jump to conclusions about Goth teenagers in general or about that individual. Or you can ask yourself, *What's behind the response I get when I use that same joke in that context as compared to when I use it at the home office?*

CQ Strategy is critical for a number of reasons. First, the conscious planning of your approach for a different context invokes creativity and innovation rather than simply relying on the same old practices that work in your familiar context. Second, the conscious attempt to be aware promotes active thinking about whether your plan was appropriate for a particular situation. And checking helps you continually revise and innovate as you monitor the effectiveness of what you're doing.

CQ STRATEGY PRACTICES

1. *Practice the "Why, Why, Why?" strategy.* By repeatedly asking ourselves "Why?" (five is a good rule of thumb), we get to the deeper levels of an issue.[7] It might look something like this:

   • We still don't have a contract from Japan. *Why?*

   • They wouldn't sign it before we left. *Why?*

   • They're uncomfortable that Susan is no longer managing the account. *Why?*

   • Trust among Japanese leaders takes a long time. *Why?*

   • Because trust is built on relationships, not just signed documents. *Why?*

   Beware of asking others the "why" question because it can make them defensive. But using it personally can be very effective.

2. *Keep a journal of your intercultural reflections.* It can be as basic as writing and checking your explanations for something like the picture in Figure 6-1. Or it can be a matter of describing your cross-cultural interactions and listing the corresponding questions and insights. Go back later and reread what you wrote. Do this with some of your colleagues and discuss the insights together.[8]

3. *Examine cross-cultural situations in what you see and read.* When reading professional journals and newspapers or simply watching a movie, observe intercultural scenarios and think of ways you would work through those situations. Don't try to resolve them too quickly but practice becoming aware, developing a plan, and then finding ways to check the appropriateness of your plans.

4. *Engage in active planning.* When you take on a new assignment that involves a high level of intercultural engagement, think about how your approach will differ from how you would do this assignment with people from your own culture. Find someone to run this by who can offer informed input.

5. *Find cultural guides.* When working extensively with a particular culture, find someone to be your coach. Select guides carefully. Some things to look for are as follows:

- Can they distinguish what's different about this culture from others?

- Do they demonstrate self-awareness? Other-awareness?

- Are they familiar with your culture, including your national culture and your vocational culture (e.g., engineering or health care)?

- Have they worked across numerous cultures themselves?

- Do they ask lots of questions or simply "tell" you?

- Can they articulate what kinds of personalities often get most frustrated in this culture?

A cultural guide with a good measure of multicultural awareness will serve you well. One of the greatest things a guide can do is help you know what kinds of questions you should ask of yourself and others as you move into an assignment.

CHAPTER 7

CQ ACTION: BE YOURSELF, SORT OF

CQ ACTION: What behaviors do I need to adjust?	
Changing verbal and nonverbal actions appropriately when interacting cross-culturally	
Profile of a leader with high CQ Action	Leaders with high CQ Action can draw on the other three capabilities of CQ to translate their enhanced motivation, understanding, and planning into action. They possess a broad repertoire of behaviors, which they can use depending on the context.

Two years ago, Simon left his role as a CEO of a growing company in Chicago and became president of a small, private liberal arts college in New England. The college has enjoyed a long reputation for offering an excellent liberal arts education but has been at a plateau for the last decade. The organizational structure is inflexible, enrollment is in decline, and the college has very little ethnic diversity among its faculty, staff, and students. Simon and the college seemed like a perfect match. Education is something Simon has always valued, not the least of which is evident from his PhD in business from the University of Chicago. He thrives on coming in and reinventing an organization. He's an innovator, a charismatic leader, and naturally curious about different cultures given his own Chinese American heritage. I met Simon when he agreed to be part of my research on cultural intelligence among academic leaders. Simon describes himself as a Type A, obsessive-compulsive leader. He's a fitness buff, his clothes are always neatly pressed, and his office is meticulously tidy. His magnetic smile matches his contagious personality.

Simon described his first two years at the college as the hardest assignment he had ever been given. This was no small statement coming from him. The last company he led filed for bankruptcy just before he arrived. In less than three years, he led a turnaround resulting in the company's most profitable year over its twenty-five-year history. And the business he led prior to that was also in crisis before he came in and quickly gave it a bright, new future. But Simon had met his match. There were way too few results from his first twenty-four months leading the college. Although the financial picture was more sound and enrollment had at least held steady, that was far from the kind of performance Simon was used to.

Simon had a decent understanding of the academic subculture. He knew he couldn't just apply the same kinds of leadership approaches at the college that he used in the corporate world. And although the New England community where he was now living had less ethnic diversity than he had ever experienced in his life, he had always been able to adapt to new cultural surroundings. Simon was highly motivated to see the college thrive, and he drew on his understanding of business and education to develop a plan for turning around the college's flat numbers. But there was something that kept him from feeling like he was really leading effectively, which was unlike anything he had ever experienced as a leader.

While I was visiting Simon at his college, he invited me to sit in on a personnel meeting in which he was giving an update and casting vision for the future. Just a few minutes into Simon's presentation, I was captivated. His content was substantive, he offered some humor, and he communicated an inspiring vision for the college. I was almost ready to ask him for a job! I looked around and began to wonder why there were so many blank stares. The faculty and staff couldn't have looked more bored and disengaged. If I had been speaking, their glassy eyes would have sucked the life out of me. But Simon kept at it. If anything, his charisma and delivery seemed to become more ramped up the longer he spoke.

Possessing the motivation to run at a challenge like the one facing Simon is extremely important (CQ Drive). Furthermore, having knowledge about the various cultures where you lead is essential—including the organizational culture and the various national and ethnic cultures represented (CQ Knowledge). And it is a must to have the ability to draw on that understanding to plan and accurately interpret what is going on (CQ Strategy). But, ultimately, you need to ask yourself, *Can I effectively lead in this context? Can I motivate this group toward a shared outcome and can I do so effectively and authentically?* Our individual leadership is ultimately judged based on whether or not we bring about results.

The final step toward cultural intelligence, CQ Action, is where the rubber meets the road. Do we know what someone is talking about? Are we able to communicate effectively? Can we lead people respectfully and adjust our behavior as needed while still remaining true to who we are? CQ Action is the extent to which we *appropriately* change our verbal and nonverbal actions when we interact across cultures. The goal is to be yourself while figuring out which behaviors need to change in order to accomplish your objectives. As noted at the beginning of the book, one of the revolutionary aspects of the cultural intelligence model is the emphasis on inward transformation in our perspective and outlook rather than just trying to master the "dos" and avoid the taboos. Artificial attempts to modify behavior invite inflexibility and fall short of giving us a sustainable approach to leading cross-culturally.[1] The degree to which we continue to change internally will be seen in the impressions we leave on others through our actions.

Ironically, the most effective way to adapt our behavior is through the other three capabilities of CQ. CQ Action is primarily the outcome of our CQ Drive, Knowledge, and Strategy. In one sense, this whole book is about CQ Action because our behavior is really the only way someone will know whether we're culturally intelligent. But there are a few specific leadership behaviors we need to be able to adapt when necessary. CQ Action includes three subdimensions: speech acts, verbal behavior, and nonverbal behavior.[2] These subdimensions inform the ways we can develop our CQ Action as leaders. CQ Action can be enhanced by adapting our communication, adjusting our leadership performance, and knowing when to adapt and when *not* to adapt.

Adapt Your Communication

In Chapter 4 (CQ Knowledge), we noted the importance of language for effective leadership. Whether casting vision, building trust, giving directions, or addressing conflict, a great deal centers

HOW TO DEVELOP CQ ACTION

1. Adapt your communication.
2. Lead differently.
3. Know when to adapt and when not to adapt.

Key question: What behaviors should I adapt for this cross-cultural project?

around whether we can get the message across effectively, clearly, and respectfully. Communication is not only about saying the right thing. It's about the right thing being understood. Nearly every book on leadership includes a section on the importance of communication. For me, Simon's communication was lucid and compelling. But it appeared that the faculty and staff he was leading didn't receive his message the same way I did. As I interviewed some of them, I found they weren't nearly as inspired by Simon's vision casting as I was. The recurring response from faculty when asked to describe Simon's leadership was that he was an outsider who was trying to turn the college into a business. Several professors were unnerved by the way Simon continually used words such as *bottom line, enterprise,* and *capitalize.* This was proof to them that Simon didn't understand the academic world. And given that he often referenced stories from his corporate background and frequently cited University of Phoenix as a success story, his impassioned, articulate presentations made little impact on them.[3] Some of the staff had responses similar to those of the faculty, but a more common theme in their feedback was their perception that Simon's constant enthusiasm was inauthentic. Most of the staff members at the college were native to New England, and listening to a public speaker with so much energy and charisma caused them to feel like Simon was trying to sell them something. They couldn't get beyond the sense that his delivery was a contrived performance rather than just a talk with them as colleagues. One woman even characterized him as a "used car salesman," a derogatory slur to suggest Simon was trying to swindle and manipulate the collegiate community. The cultural realities of this New England college were in conflict with the ways Simon had always communicated as a leader. We often miss the cultural differences that exist right within our own borders. No one at Simon's college referenced his Asian background as a roadblock. But his corporate, Midwest background seemed to be a huge roadblock for them.

The ability to communicate effectively in a new cultural context demonstrates how CQ Action becomes the natural outgrowth of the other three CQ capabilities. A level of motivation and energy (CQ Drive) is needed to relearn how to communicate in ways that build trust and motivate people in a new context. A great deal of understanding (CQ Knowledge) is also needed to know what cultural systems and values are utilized and the words to use and avoid. And a heightened level of planning, awareness, and checking (CQ Strategy) is necessary to actually communicate relevant ideas. There are three communication behaviors that most need our attention when communicating in a different cultural context: word usage, delivery, and nonverbal actions.[4]

Word Usage

The very words that create vision and expectation in one cultural context can elicit distrust and suspicion in another. I can think of several people from many contexts who would have listened to Simon's presentation and found it inspiring and right on the mark. But that's not how it was received by his college personnel. It doesn't really matter if I was inspired by Simon. His team wasn't!

There are a few different ways to think about how we use words when we lead cross-culturally: topics, requests, apologies, and compliments.

TOPICS

Appropriately adapting our behavior involves learning what topics of discussion are appropriate in various settings. Although this applies to work-related conversations, it's most apparent in more informal, social interactions. Earlier, I noted that the after-hours drink with someone from a different cultural background is often far more challenging than interactions revolving around work. Yet these informal interactions are often the more important ones.

Sometimes people from other cultures have asked me during an informal conversation how much money I make or how much my home costs, questions that would be considered off limits even among close friends in my cultural context. And I've been with colleagues who have been told they're looking very "fat," a description I've taught my kids to never use in reference to anyone. But these topics might not be considered disrespectful at all in other cultures. In fact, being told you're fat in many African cultures is a real compliment. It's evidence you're wealthy and successful. Other times I've been the one who has come across as rude. I've asked single friends from other cultures about their love lives only to learn I was being too forward according to their cultural norms. Or I've neglected to ask about their families or share more about mine.

There are many other examples. Religion and politics are typically seen as off limits among North American colleagues unless there's a clear invitation to discuss these subjects. But many Germans value overt expressions of opinion on these kinds of topics in order to have a good argumentative exchange. For Germans, getting to know someone means finding out what the other person's positions are on different issues and debating them as a means of interaction. In contrast, when Chinese individuals meet for the first time, their approach for getting to know each other is usually quite different. Instead of heated dialogue and debating each other, you usually start by talking about your family background and asking others about theirs. Only after that kind of rapport is developed is it appropriate to discuss social and political issues. North Americans and Japanese often talk about business long into the dinner hour but British individuals tend to think shop talk needs to stop once the workday is over. Different conventions for selecting conversational strategies and topics are an area of behavior we may need to adapt.[5]

Few things demonstrate the cultural variance of conversational protocol more than humor. Jokes and things we find funny often depend on an assumed understanding and history. I was recently on a flight sitting next to a Chinese American businesswoman. She travels regularly to China to translate for English-speaking corporate trainers who conduct seminars there. She commented on how most of the U.S. and British trainers with whom she works start their presentations with a joke or humorous anecdote. This is an approach that seems to work well for them in their own context. But my seatmate told me that when they do that in China, instead of translating what they're saying, she says to the Mandarin-speaking audience, "Our presenter is telling a joke right now. The polite thing to do will be to laugh when he's done." Humor is deeply rooted in cultural assumptions, whether used in public speaking or interpersonal conversation.

Culturally intelligent leaders understand that topics discussed, particularly in social, informal settings, are embedded with cultural values and assumptions. Discernment in how to use words begins with considering appropriate conversation topics and effective use of small talk.

REQUESTS

Helen Spencer-Oatey, a renowned linguistic researcher, describes the cultural variances in how we make a request of someone. Individuals coming from cultures where indirect communication is valued, such as China, will often use the power of suggestion to make a request. However, people from the United States or Israel will usually be more direct with orders and requests. Think about the progression from a very direct to a very indirect approach to asking an employee to run a budget report:

- "Run the budget report!"
- "I want you to run the budget report."
- "How about running the budget report?"
- "Can you run the budget report?"
- "Wouldn't it help to have a budget report?"[6]

Leaders have to learn the level of comfort individuals and cultures have with direct versus indirect orders and requests and adjust accordingly. There's further variance in how this communication practice relates to a culture's value of power distance. A culture that values indirect communication may also be a place where senior leaders give explicit and direct orders to subordinates if there's a high level of power distance (e.g., a Chinese boss is likely to be very direct with an assistant about running a budget report). But a subordinate would be expected to use extremely indirect communication to make a request of a superior. Peers are expected to use indirect communication with one another lest it seem one is taking on an authoritative role over the other. You need to learn where you're perceived in the hierarchical structure to gauge the appropriate level of directness to employ.

Suzanne, a North American expatriate working in France, discovered the importance of how she made a request when she went shopping in Paris. Suzanne is fluent in French but that didn't mitigate the challenges she felt in communicating. Early on during her sojourn in France, she couldn't seem to get beyond her perception that French people disliked Americans in general. Whenever she asked for something specific of a shopkeeper, such as "Where can I find the lipstick?" she received a curt, abrupt response. One day, a French friend suggested, "Try starting with something like

Humble yourself !

this when you walk into the store: 'Could you help me with a problem?' And if they say 'Yes'—which they more than likely will—then ask for help finding the lipstick." Suzanne tried it and she couldn't believe how well it worked. It changed the whole disposition of the shopkeepers because now she was posturing herself as someone in need rather than someone making demands. She began to apply the same kind of strategy with her colleagues and subordinates at work. She was amazed at how this simple adjustment altered the way her requests were received. Simply understanding some basic shifts in language can make all the difference in achieving our objectives, whether it's to purchase lipstick or to launch a full-orbed initiative.[7]

The most important phrase I try to learn in the language spoken any place I visit is "I'm sorry, I don't speak _____. Do you speak English?" It postures me as being in need rather than presuming everyone would be happy to help in English. Even if I can't say it in the local language, asking first whether someone speaks English demonstrates that I don't simply assume they should and instead, postures me as a foreign guest who needs help.

APOLOGIES

Another communication challenge is knowing when and how to apologize. People in most cultures would agree that an apology of some sort is needed when an offense occurs. The question is, What's considered offensive and what's the most appropriate way to express regret for an offense?

Growing up in a Canadian home, "Sorry" was something we said all the time, given a predominant thrust across Canadian culture to never impose upon others. I've often said "Sorry!" for bumping into people in places like Brazil only to have them look at me as if to say, *Sorry for what?!* To invade one's personal space is a violation in my culture but close proximity and sharing personal space is a part of life for many Brazilians. It's important to learn when and how you should apologize to a colleague given his or her culture. An individual coming from a polychronic culture might see little offense in being an hour late to a meeting, but a culturally intelligent individual will understand that keeping someone from a monochronic culture waiting for an hour requires an apology. In the mind of most people from monochronic cultures, to keep others waiting for an hour is to have wasted their time and disrespects them. On the other hand, abruptly ending a conversation with someone from a polychronic culture in order to get to an appointment may be something that requires an apology. And in cultures where hierarchy is important, a lower-status individual is expected to offer deference and an apologetic posture to someone with higher status, even if no great offense has occurred. An outsider need not mimic all these behaviors, something we'll address later in the chapter, but we'd be wise to understand the importance of these kinds of communication practices.

Korean advertising through email often begins with the sentence "I am sorry to send you spam." A spam message with an apology is deemed more credible in the Korean context but would be seen as a position of weakness to a North American audience. Learn when and how to apologize to the people in the cultures with which you regularly work.

In 2001, a U.S. surveillance plane and a Chinese fighter jet collided over the South China Sea. The next several days resulted in heated arguments between U.S. and Chinese diplomats over whether the U.S. government should apologize. The Chinese Ministry of Foreign Affairs insisted that the U.S. government accept full responsibility. Viewing the aggressiveness of the Chinese fighter jet as the reason for the collision, U.S. Secretary of State Colin Powell refused to issue an apology. His response aligned with the typical U.S. view of apologies. An apology is rooted in a pragmatic understanding of who is at fault. The emphasis of an apology is in looking for responsibility for something done. The

Chinese view is oriented around harmony and a bigger view of the circumstances. The emphasis is on a willingness to acknowledge the unfortunate event rather than precisely who was at fault. The Chinese were angered not so much by the incident of a U.S. plane being in their airspace but in the unwillingness to issue an apology.[8] As we become more aware of cultural values (individualism versus collectivism, or particularism versus universalism), CQ Strategy helps us translate that understanding into appropriate ways to give and receive apologies.

COMPLIMENTS

The giving and receiving of compliments is another communication exercise that requires cultural intelligence. When complimented, should you acknowledge it or is it better to deflect it to avoid seeming self-congratulatory? And when you want to encourage a colleague or subordinate, is it best to compliment the individual publicly, privately, or not at all? Is a compliment best expressed through words, gifts, or another approach? In many Western cultures, it's largely agreed that the best way to respond to a compliment is simply to accept it. However, the reverse is true in many Eastern cultures. Rejection or denial of a compliment is deemed more appropriate in places like Japan and China. Of course, this is another example where there are plenty of individual differences among people who share a culture depending on their personality and family upbringing, hence the need for awareness, planning, and checking (CQ Strategy) as we compliment and affirm individuals.

A leader might presume a compliment will motivate a subordinate to continue good work; but if the individual perceives a boss as being too personal and reflecting more intimacy in their relationship than appropriate, it might actually play a demotivating role. And leaders from individualist cultures often single out high-performing staff members and publicly acknowledge them.

But that can bring about embarrassment and shame for someone in a collectivist culture who has been taught to never stand out. On the other hand, leaders in collectivist cultures who offer little personalized affirmation and encouragement to colleagues and clients from individualist cultures can be seen as ungrateful.

Leaders can't expect to master all the norms for appropriate compliments for every culture they'll encounter. But they'd be well advised to understand and practice basic adaptive behavior in how they can offer encouragement and praise to people from different cultural backgrounds. An overall posture of respect and suspended judgment will help leaders grow in knowing the appropriate way to communicate gratitude and affirm success.

Effective leadership is highly dependent on the exchange of words. The greatest challenge exists when different languages are spoken in the same work environment. Leaders who are willing to learn new languages or learn to use translators are needed. But anytime we communicate cross-culturally, even when there's a shared language, basic communication behaviors like those covered will play a strong role in how we lead.

Delivery

As important as words are, it wasn't only Simon's words that made the faculty and staff at his college uncomfortable. It was also the way he delivered them. Even when appropriate words are chosen, how the information is delivered can cause a great deal of miscommunication. Culturally intelligent leaders will learn what communication is best offered in writing, when to pick up the phone, and when to communicate face-to-face. They will gain confidence in knowing the appropriate level of enthusiasm, pace, and style to use when talking to different audiences. Although leaders in low power distance cultures can use the same style of communication when interacting with an administrative assistant as with a vice president, that isn't so in high power distance cultures. We'll explore several of the nonverbal dimensions of communication separately in just a minute, but it's important to specifically address the manner in which words are spoken, or the delivery.

Many native-English speakers fail to alter their delivery when communicating with individuals for whom English is a second language. This is something I'm continually working on myself. Growing up in New York, I was socialized to speak quickly, get to the point, and express enthusiasm when appropriate. I have to continually work on slowing down, especially when speaking publicly to non-native English speakers. Here are several strategies for enhancing communication when addressing an audience including non-native English speakers:

- Slow down. Slow down. Slow down. Slllllloooooowwwwww d o w n.
- Use clear, slow speech. Enunciate carefully.
- Avoid colloquial expressions and idioms.
- Repeat important points using different words to explain the same thing.
- Avoid long, compound sentences.
- Use visual representations (pictures, tables, graphs, etc.) to support what is being said.
- Mix presentations with a balance of story and principles.
- Hand out written summaries.
- Pause more frequently.

Most of these same strategies apply to small-group and one-on-one communication too. We have to find the delivery style that is most comfortable to us so it appears natural and authentic. But we also have to learn what kinds of alterations to make to our "natural" style when addressing various audiences. Simon needed to find a way to use the public-speaking style most comfortable to him while also adjusting for the New England, academic subculture where he was leading. Then, as we learn to alter our delivery, we have to continually check for understanding. It's not enough to simply ask, "Are you with me? Does this make sense?" Instead, we have to create questions and activities that will reveal the level of understanding among those listening, or find a cultural coach to help us check whether our plan worked.

Nonverbal Actions

We've all heard it said, "You cannot not communicate." Although words and delivery are an important part of the communication exchange, as much and possibly more gets communicated through other nonverbal behaviors. It's important to note a few of the ways culture affects nonverbal behavior, including distance, touching, body position, gestures, facial expressions, and eye contact.

DISTANCE

Many of us have felt the discomfort that comes from someone violating what we consider to be appropriate personal space. Culture plays a huge role in what we view as appropriate distance. The average conversation distance preferred by most in the Anglo cluster is fifty centimeters (twenty inches), whereas for the Latin clusters it's closer to thirty-five centimeters (fourteen inches) and for the Arab cluster it's twenty-five centimeters (ten inches). When Arabs overstep the preferred personal space of Anglos, it's often viewed as intrusive or aggressive, and when Anglos keep their distance, Arabs often perceive this behavior as cold and aloof.[9] The amount of space between seats when conducting a training session, the way an office is set up, and the way a boss interacts with staff are all ways distance influences the ways we behave cross-culturally. Be alert regarding how social distance affects your interactions and be prepared to modify it.[10]

TOUCHING

The handshake, though most widely used in Western contexts, has been broadly accepted in professional settings around the world as an appropriate greeting. But the degree of firmness, the appropriate duration of the contact, and the individual who initiates it vary widely from one cultural context to another. In many settings, it's considered rude if you don't shake the hand of each person standing together—beginning with the person of highest status. And putting a hand on another person's back or shoulder is appropriate in some professional settings and not others. It is important to consider different levels of authority, gender, and age when determining appropriate touching. For example, individuals from many high power distance cultures have expectations about how handshakes should occur between individuals according to their status. When greeting someone with higher status, the lower status individual is expected to support his wrist with his left hand while shaking hands. Many African cultures use a more gentle handshake than is commonly used in Europe or the United States but linger while holding the other person's hand. Such cues are important for leading in many situations. Pay attention to these actions when observing others as well as in your own interactions. It's generally agreed that cultures with the lowest amount of touching are found in North America, Northern Europe, and Asia. Cultures with a high amount of touching are found in Latin America, Southern and Eastern Europe, and the Middle East. As always, beware of individual differences that exist among people in various contexts.

BODY POSITION

There are unwritten, often even unconscious cultural rules that govern the degree to which individuals sit, stand, and bow. In some contexts, people's gender, age, and level of authority all determine where they should position themselves in relation to others. And bowing is a key nonverbal behavior used in many contexts like

Japan, Korea, and Thailand. The unwritten rules about bowing in places like these are complex and very difficult for an outsider to master. Rather than become overwhelmed by this, the culturally intelligent leader knows that certain body positions are best reserved for those who practice them. But we're wise to consider which of our postures should be altered.

GESTURES

People often use gestures to accompany things they're saying. It's especially difficult to understand gestures if you don't understand the language. And gestures are one of the most highly individualized forms of communication. So although there are some cultural norms, CQ Strategy is needed to discern whether a gesture is a reflection of a culture or of an individual. Watch for cues. For example, notice how someone uses a gesture such as pointing. Then observe whether others from the same cultural context use this gesture. I've inadvertently sent the wrong message by placing my hands in my pockets during an international presentation, implying an overly casual or even disrespectful posture to some cultures. Test your assumptions and be very cautious before enacting new gestures just because you've observed them in others.

FACIAL EXPRESSIONS

Facial expressions can be highly misleading, as evidenced by international volunteers who assume smiling faces by poor people mean they're happy. On the other hand, I've often heard Westerners look at a photo of an Indian family and ask why everyone is so serious and no one is smiling. Review the differences described in Chapter 5 between neutral and affective cultures and practice saying the same thing with varying levels of facial expressiveness. Accurately understanding the meaning behind others' facial expressions is one of the most subjective challenges we'll encounter. Use extreme caution in making judgments about what a facial expression means when observed cross-culturally. But try some slight adjustments in your own levels of expressiveness as you interact from one culture to the next.

EYE CONTACT

The final important nonverbal behavior to adapt is eye contact. Different cultures have various norms about when and how long eye contact is appropriate. This becomes further complicated because most cultures have unwritten rules about how to use eye contact according to gender, age, and status. One day I talked to a manager who said everything about a job candidate suggested she should hire him. But he wouldn't look her in the eye, which made her distrust him. I asked her what his cultural background was. "He's Saudi," she said. Though Arabs often have conventions of longer eye contact than some other cultures do, many Saudi men have been socialized to avoid direct eye contact with women. Most Arabs, Latinos, Indians, and Pakistanis have conventions of longer eye contact, whereas Africans and East Asians interpret too much direct eye contact as conveying anger or insubordination and prefer to avoid it.[11]

Many people want a simple list of the dos and don'ts of behavior for any culture in the world. To rely on such information can be risky because of the many subjective elements that go along with behavioral practices (e.g., the gender, age, or status of the person involved; whether an individual is like his or her cultural background). However, if you're encountering a culture for the first time, this kind of information can be a useful starting point. The bestselling book *Kiss, Bow, or Shake Hands* by Terri Morrison and Wayne Conaway provides helpful information, but use it carefully, lest you resort to stereotypes. The best book I've read on a more culturally intelligent approach to adapting behavior is Andy Molinsky's *Global Dexterity.* I highly recommend adding both of these books to your library.

As you know by now, the goal isn't to become an expert on the perfect word, delivery, or nonverbal behavior for every situation. Instead, the key is the ability to accurately observe the behavior of others, reflect on it, and learn when to modify your actions in response.

Lead Differently

Throughout the book we've been talking about how to adjust your leadership based on the cultures involved. But what does it look like to have high CQ Action as a leader? Rather than describe this generically, let's look at one specific task that nearly all of us are required to do as leaders—negotiation—as an example of CQ Action applied to leadership. Whether it's negotiating with the board, government officials, staff, or customers, effective negotiation is a crucial leadership skill used on a daily basis. Regardless of the cultural context, the objective in negotiation is for people to reach an agreement that mutually satisfies their respective interests, both personally and organizationally. Effective negotiations usually include offers and counteroffers with concessions and compromises along the way before reaching an agreement.[12]

The cultural values we reviewed in Chapter 5 directly influence how negotiations occur. Jeswald Salacuse, author of *The Global Negotiator,* draws on this material and his own research to suggest ten questions to consider when negotiating across cultures.[13]

1. Negotiating Goal: Contract or Relationship?

For some cultures, partnering implies building a relationship, whereas for others it's primarily a contractual transaction. Determine the goal as soon as possible. If you're trying to partner with relationally driven negotiators and you are highlighting most your ability to deliver a low-cost contract, it can cost you the deal. For those who primarily want a contract, trying to build a relationship may be viewed as pandering and wasting their time.

2. Negotiating Attitude: Win–Lose or Win–Win?

Many negotiation books presume everyone is after a win-win; however, some cultures and organizations are driven by an approach that assumes one side wins and the other side loses. Win-win negotiators see deal making as a collaborative, problem-solving process, whereas win-lose negotiators view it as confrontational. Your CQ Action will come through in your ability to deal with either kind of negotiator.

3. Personal Style: Informal or Formal?

Some cultures prefer a formal style of negotiation that emphasizes titles and avoids discussions about personal matters. For example, Koreans are typically described as having a much more formal negotiation style than North Americans. North American negotiators often try to start the discussion on a first-name basis and to put everyone at ease by engaging in small talk. It's easier and safer to begin with a more formal approach and move toward a more informal one when it becomes evident that the culture and situation allow for it.

4. Communication: Direct or Indirect?

In cultures that rely on indirect communication, such as many of the Confucian Asian cultures, an initial meeting will rarely disclose a definite commitment or rejection. Indirect negotiators are wise to recognize that their direct counterparts may not accurately understand what's occurring if it isn't explicitly stated. Without cultural intelligence, negotiations that involve direct and indirect communicators often result in direct communicators interpreting the behavior of indirect counterparts as passive aggressive and unable to make a decision, and indirect communicators perceiving direct negotiators as aggressive and pushy.

5. Sensitivity to Time: High or Low?

Different perceptions regarding time is typically the area of greatest conflict in intercultural negotiations. In many Asian and Latino cultures, it's impossible to conceive of reaching an agreement without spending significant time getting to know each other. In these cultures, building relationships requires that negotiators take time to learn about the people with whom they are negotiating. Ways to do this include going out for dinner or drinks, visiting national landmarks, playing golf, or going to a cricket game. This type of ritual socializing is vital because it represents an honest effort to understand as fully as possible the needs, values, and interests of the other side. In contrast, many Western European and North American cultures value expediency in reaching a deal. For these individuals, vast amounts of time socializing can seem like a disregard for the value of one's time. McDonald's took nearly a decade to negotiate with Russian leaders in Moscow before selling burgers there. Adjust your expectations and approach for the amount of time and type of relationship required to negotiate. It almost always takes longer to negotiate across borders.

6. Emotionalism: High or Low?

To what degree should negotiations involve wearing people down emotionally? Affective cultures (described in Chapter 5) such as Latin Europe are more likely to show their emotions at the negotiating table, whereas neutral cultures such as the Dutch and Japanese are unlikely to disclose their feelings toward the deal. Start more neutral and follow your counterpart's lead.

7. Form of Agreement: General or Specific?

Cultural variations will influence the way both parties believe the deal should be written. North Americans typically prefer detailed contracts that anticipate all kinds of circumstances so that the contract can be used to handle any kind of situation that arises. However, a lot of other cultures, such as with many Chinese, prefer a contract in the form of general assumptions and guidelines, believing that the agreement is primarily the relationship between two parties, not an abstract document. Using this more general approach, the parties should look primarily to their relationship, not the contract, to solve unexpected problems.

8. Building an Agreement: Bottom Up or Top Down?

Whether the value for the other side is in starting with agreement on general principles (top down) or with specifics (bottom up) needs to be determined in intercultural negotiations. Salacuse suggests that the French prefer to begin with agreement on general principles, whereas North Americans begin with agreement on specific deliverables and develop the general principles based on those deliverables. An organization's culture and the individual personalities involved also play a significant role in whether a bottom-up or top-down approach works. As you apply your CQ Action to negotiation, you'll be better served to negotiate in familiar cultures too.

On a related note, Salacuse distinguishes between "building-up" and "building-down" negotiation styles. He states:

> In the building down approach, the negotiator begins by presenting the maximum deal if the other side accepts all the stated conditions. In the building-up approach, one side begins by proposing a minimum deal that can be broadened and increased as the other party accepts additional conditions. According to many observers, Americans tend to favor the building-down ap-

proach, while the Japanese tend to prefer the building-up style of negotiating a contract.[14]

9. Team Organization: One Leader or Group Consensus?

Any effective negotiation requires learning who ultimately makes the decisions and how the authority structure works. But this isn't always easy to determine when negotiating across cultures. Many collectivist cultures will have large groups show up for a negotiation meeting while many others not at the table may also be involved in reaching consensus. And many individualist cultures expect that one or two key individuals will ultimately be the ones who make the decision. Don't assume you know who the decision maker is. Use your CQ Knowledge and Strategy to figure it out.

10. Risk Taking: High or Low?

Finally, you'll want to understand where the organization and individuals fall on the uncertainty avoidance dimension. Those from high uncertainty avoidance cultures such as Israel and Japan will often want much more information and detailed processes to help alleviate uncertainty. In contrast, those from low uncertainty avoidance cultures may feel distrusted and frustrated if there's an overemphasis on endless "what if" scenarios.

As you listen and negotiate, beware of an overreliance on cultural stereotypes. As always, they're a good first guess, but they can derail your entire negotiation process when applied too broadly or mindlessly. You have to use the awareness of CQ Strategy to get below the surface of the iceberg and attend to the specific individuals and organization involved. Simultaneously, you need to remain alert to how you're being viewed. What kind of preconceptions do the people you are negotiating with have given your cultural background or previous experiences? How will you need to compensate for those perceptions?

Once you have a negotiation plan in mind, hold it loosely and be ready to adapt. Anticipate ahead of time where you are willing to adjust. You don't want to make concessions you'll later regret but you also don't want to lose the deal because of inflexibility. In the midst of the negotiation, draw on the skills developed in CQ Strategy to stay alert to what's going on behind the scenes in the negotiating process. I wouldn't even consider entering a cross-cultural negotiation without a cultural broker to help me interpret what's going on. Find someone you trust who can help you make sense of what various tactics mean.

Negotiation exemplifies how CQ Action influences leadership performance. It requires an ability to adapt without abandoning the interests of yourself and your organization. Negotiation across borders requires all four CQ capabilities. Be ready to adapt the way you negotiate as you work in various contexts.

Know When to Adapt and When Not to Adapt

Should we always adapt to the other culture, and who adapts to whom? Too much adaptation can generate suspicion and distrust, yet inflexible behavior is a sure death wish for most twenty-first-century leaders and organizations. When should we alter our strategy, and when should it remain unchanged? When is it okay to pass on eating something that turns our stomach, and when should we eat and pray, "Dear God, help me keep it down"? As we broaden our repertoire of cultural understanding and behavior, we'll become more attuned to knowing which response is appropriate.

Learning if and when it's appropriate to adapt our behavior to another culture is a complex area. It's more than just knowing the behavior of people from other cultures. It requires drawing on CQ Knowledge and CQ Strategy to anticipate what people from other cultures expect of us as well as the consequences of adapting or not.

There are some situations in which the best option is to *not* adapt at all. Adjusting to the behavior of another culture is a double-edged sword. Some level of adapting to communication styles and patterns cross-culturally is usually viewed positively because it leads to perceptions of similarity. However, high levels of adaptation are viewed negatively. Extensive mimicry can be seen as insincere and possibly even deceptive.[15] Individuals who "go native" and try to entirely strip themselves of their own culture can be seen as trying too hard. Uncritically accepting everything in a new culture and turning one's back on one's own birth culture is not culturally intelligent behavior.

I've sometimes observed adults overadapting when working with adolescents. Youth are usually grateful for adult teachers and coaches who try to understand and respect their interests. But that doesn't mean they want their teachers to start dressing like them and going to the same concerts. There's nothing worse than seeing a fifty-year-old coach dress and act like a fifteen-year-old. Likewise, in most places, it's viewed as humorous and downright silly when outsiders try to wear native dress. Women dressing more modestly than they might at home or men dressing more or less formally according to the cultural norm is appropriate. But going fully native in our dress isn't usually the way to go. Similarly, if you're invited to participate at a conference in Japan, most Japanese will be favorably impressed if you're courteous, polite, and somewhat reserved. But they don't expect you to master the intricate social skills of Japan such as bowing in all the appropriate ways. In fact, if you try to mimic cultures like these too much, at best your behavior will be seen as amusing, and more likely it will be seen as offensive.

How do we know whether to adapt or not? I always ask two primary questions when trying to decide whether to adapt:

1. Is this a tight or loose culture?

   "Tight versus loose" refers to how strong the social norms are within a given culture. Tight cultures are places where there are very prescribed expectations of how people should behave. Places like Saudi Arabia and Japan are very tight cultures because there's a predominant view on what kind of behavior is and isn't appropriate. Loose cultures are typically more cosmopolitan, and in order to absorb the heterogeneous makeup of a place, these societies are less dogmatic about what kind of behavior is acceptable. Nations like Thailand and the Netherlands are loose cultures.[16]

   If you're a woman traveling to Saudi Arabia, you need not spend much time wondering whether or not you should adapt to wearing an abaya. You should—it's the law! As a tight culture, there are very clear standards about how you should dress and behave. And while Japanese culture might not be quite as tight as Saudi Arabia's, veering from the protocols of acceptable behavior will be a much bigger deal in Tokyo than in London, a loose culture.

2. Will adapting compromise my organization or me?

   I have a set of values and convictions that I'm not willing to compromise just to fit in with another culture. I suspect the same is true for you. Some people would be compromising their health or religious beliefs by participating in the excessive drinking that sometimes occurs at Chinese business dinners. And some companies, such as Bloomberg, forbid employees from accepting gifts of any kind, including having dinner paid for, lest it compromise journalistic integrity. That policy runs against the grain of the cultural values of hospitality and gift giving in many places around the world.

But cultural intelligence is not simply play acting and performing based on others' preferences and expectations. It has to be rooted in a strong sense of yourself. You need an inner compass to help you discern when adapting goes beyond your core values. Rather than simply mimic the behaviors you observe, you need to base your decision to adapt on the knowledge of the other culture, the expectations of the people, and the objectives that need to be accomplished.

After answering these two primary questions, it's a matter of anticipating the consequences of adapting or not. You have every right to refuse to adapt to the cultural norm of after-hours binge-drinking sessions with prospective clients, but given the importance of that routine for some cultures, you'd better think about ways you can work hard to adapt in other ways (e.g., eating whatever is put in front of you). I respect Bloomberg's policy to refuse anyone treating you to dinner, but there should then be an understanding that this might make *guanxi* (the connections and resulting obligations between two individuals) harder to establish.

With experience and growing levels of cultural intelligence, our sense of if and how much to adapt may become so well developed that we adapt naturally without much conscious thought. That's the goal. We want to get to a point where this high level of thinking and action happens as naturally as the thoughts and behaviors enacted in our familiar cultural contexts. And getting there might be as simple as trial and error. Try adapting a bit and see what happens. Test it in lots of different situations. Ask a trusted peer who understands the cultural context how adapting or not adapting will be perceived by others. Then ask someone else. Then ask yet another person.

Behavior is ambiguous. The same action can have many different meanings depending on who does it, where, and with whom.

But by walking through the four capabilities of CQ, we can better discern which behaviors to adapt and those *not* to adapt.

Conclusion

My two daughters are very different from each other. Emily has always been a homebody who loves to hang out, read, talk, and share a long meal together. Grace, on the other hand, is continually moving. She's happiest when there's a lot going on. She wants to go for a bike ride, kayak on the lake together, and get coffee, maybe all in the same hour. I want to relate to my kids in ways that express my love for them. So I interact with them differently according to their unique personalities. I'm not being a chameleon. I simply want them to experience my love in ways that are meaningful to each of them.

We can't possibly learn the individual preferences of all the people we encounter in our work. But learning the cultural norms of different groups of people helps us behave more effectively and respectfully. That's why cultural intelligence is so important to me. It's an essential skill set for me as a leader to treat others with dignity and respect. And it allows me to adapt my behavior to accomplish my objectives.

CQ ACTION PRACTICES

1. *Learn what practices and taboos are most important for the key regions where you work.* Knowing when and how to exchange a business card, the protocols for gift giving, and whether or not to use the left hand are a few of the specific behaviors worth mastering. Though you can't master all the practices and taboos, you can learn which ones will most enhance or deter effectiveness.

2. *Look for consistent feedback.* Encouragement as well as corrective feedback is essential for developing CQ Action. Look for ways to get an honest assessment of your work. Both positive and negative feedback will help you to effectively enhance your ability to flex your behavior.

3. *Go together.* When you have a meeting or a trip that involves cross-cultural work, bring someone along. Processing the challenges and rewards of cross-cultural negotiation and work jointly is much more effective than doing so individually.

4. *Assess for CQ Action in all key management hires.* Hiring an increasingly diverse workforce is a vital and strategic choice, but it's not enough to simply hire more underrepresented populations. Every management position, even, and especially, positions held by individuals coming from the dominant culture, should be held by people with culturally intelligent behavior.

5. *Develop a zero-tolerance policy for inappropriate jokes and language directed toward any specific cultural group (including socio-ethnic, sexual orientation, and religious).* Encourage diversity by allowing flexibility in dress and behavior as long as it doesn't interfere with your organizational objectives.

Part III

Leveraging Cultural Intelligence

CHAPTER 8

THE ROI FOR CULTURALLY INTELLIGENT
LEADERS

Simon lasted another six months at the New England college before he decided it just wasn't a good fit. He grew significantly in his ability to see what was going on, and he was able to articulate some of the behaviors he would need to change to adapt to the school's culture. But he didn't perceive a mutual willingness to adapt to him.

As if the challenge of leading a struggling school in New England wasn't enough, Simon went on to accept the senior role at a fledgling company that provides executive coaching and training. The company had been very successful in the United States, but the last owner expanded the business into Europe and Asia and the profit margins had been in decline for the last five years. Last year, the company lost five million dollars. Simon had learned some key things about himself and the challenge of leading in various cultures—organizational, regional, and ethnic. He wanted to see if he could run at a new leadership challenge and help other leaders do the same. Over the next several months, Simon and I exchanged dozens of emails and phone calls, and we shared a few meals together. He wanted to learn more about cultural intelligence to see if he could apply it to his own leadership and to the services offered by his company.

In his direct but affable way, he said to me, "Okay, Dave, show me what the CQ research means for people like me." He had three primary questions for me:

1. What predicts someone's CQ?

2. What are the results of high CQ?

3. What's the return on investment (ROI) for organizations when improving CQ?

First, I shared with Simon the variables that predict a leader's CQ. Then we discussed the results of leading with CQ and the subsequent ROI for organizations with culturally intelligent leaders.

Predictors of Cultural Intelligence

What, if anything, predicts whether someone has cultural intelligence? Dozens of studies have been conducted across the world to investigate what personality traits and experiences are likely to influence higher CQ.[1] Keep in mind that anyone can improve his or her CQ. The emphasis of our work on cultural intelligence is more on nurture than nature. But it can be helpful to understand what personality traits are most likely to shape one's CQ. We'll review these traits followed by the kinds of experiences most likely to enhance CQ.

Personality Traits

I'm a runner. I run consistently several days a week wherever I am in the world. But there will always be people who will outrun me. Even if another runner and I use the same routine to increase our endurance and speed, our genetic makeup will play a role and my competitor may outperform me. However, I can probably outrun someone who is genetically built for running but never actually runs or exercises. The same is true for cultural intelligence. Some personality traits that are naturally built into us may predispose us to the way we relate to different cultures. But anyone can improve

CQ. How does an individual's personality influence that person's development in the four capabilities of CQ?

The Big Five model of personality traits is considered the most comprehensive research-driven inquiry into personality. The overview in Table 8-1 shows important connections between these five personality traits and the four capabilities of CQ. A "✓" signifies a positive relationship between the personality trait and the respective CQ capability (e.g., "Extraversion" predicts higher levels of CQ Drive, Knowledge, and Action, but not CQ Strategy; "Agreeableness" predicts higher levels of CQ Action but not the other three capabilities).[2]

If you do an online search for Big Five personality tests, you will find several free assessments that provide an instant self-report on your tendencies in each of these traits. This kind of understanding can help you see which CQ capabilities might come more naturally to you than others. Being an extravert is not a sure predictor of having high CQ Action. But when joined with the other ways to develop CQ, there's a positive relationship between extraversion and CQ Action. And there's a negative relationship between extraversion and CQ Knowledge and CQ Strategy. As noted in Table 8-1, openness, a curiosity about the world, is the only trait that is positively related to all four CQ capabilities. Explore the relevance of the other relationships identified in Table 8-1 for you and your team.

Experiences

There are also three experiences that consistently yield a positive relationship with higher CQ: intercultural experiences, formal education, and working in multicultural teams. These inform several of the best practices I've suggested throughout the book for enhancing cultural intelligence.

Intercultural experience by itself does not ensure cultural intelligence, but when wed with the other capabilities of cultural intelligence it plays a significant role. In particular, individuals

Table 8-1. Correlation Between Personality Traits
and Cultural Intelligence

Personality Trait	Definition	CQ Drive	CQ Knowledge	CQ Strategy	CQ Action
Extraversion	The degree to which an individual is outgoing, social, and derives energy from being with people	✓	✓		✓
Agreeableness	The degree to which an individual is cooperative and trusting				✓
Conscientiousness	The degree to which an individual is disciplined and plans			✓	
Emotional Stability	The degree to which an individual is steady and not emotional, with limited anxiety				✓
Openness to Experience	The degree to which an individual is imaginative and open to varying experiences and perspectives	✓	✓	✓	✓

with multiple experiences in a variety of places experience more of the benefits of intercultural interactions and travel than those who have been in only one or two places, even if for a long time. And the more countries where you've lived for more than a year, the more positive connection there is between your international experience and cultural intelligence.[3] In addition, individuals who are part of an underrepresented culture and have had to put concerted effort toward adapting to the dominant culture have increased opportunities for building cultural intelligence. Childhood experiences play less of a role in developing cultural intelligence than adult experiences because as adults we make our own choices about travel, work, and interactions. But no matter how old you are, the key variable is who helps you interpret the experience. If parents take their children somewhere and point out only the negative aspects of the culture, it might actually erode cultural intelligence rather than improve it. Thankfully, the reverse is also true. Parents who immerse their kids in other cultures and help them see all the differences can give their children an early start in developing cultural intelligence. If study-abroad students live on Skype and Facebook when they go overseas, or if business travelers eat their meals at the international hotel restaurant and rely on the assigned driver to take them places, the international experience may have little positive benefit for improving CQ as compared to those who venture out to find eateries and transportation on their own. When done well, intercultural experience is positively related to all four capabilities of cultural intelligence.[4]

Your education level is also positively related to cultural intelligence. Advanced training, both formal and informal, shows a positive relationship with one's overall CQ. University-level and postgraduate education, in particular, nurtures an ability to critically engage with more complex ways of perceiving the world. Despite the many fair criticisms about how formal education often fails to provide real-world knowledge, the strength of a good university education is that it requires discipline to learn new ideas, integrate them with one's own understanding and experience, and synthesize them for use in one's life and work. Therefore, not only is the content useful for expanding your cultural intelligence, but the very learning process itself is conducive to cultural analysis, interpretation, and engagement. This isn't a linear, causal relationship. There are plenty of PhDs and college graduates who have low CQ. But engaging in classes, integrative assignments, and formal education can be one of the most powerful ways to develop CQ.[5]

Finally, the degree to which you've participated in multicultural teams plays a role in helping you to adapt to various cultural situations. If you've only been on homogeneous teams, you may have limited tacit knowledge about the creativity and flexibility required to get people working together. But the more experience you have being a part of a diverse team, the better the chances of improving your CQ. Diversity is not enough. Just as international experience and education don't guarantee high CQ, diversity left to itself may actually reinforce stereotypes and frustrations about working cross-culturally. But multicultural teams offer a built-in opportunity for people to improve CQ. And if you're in an organization or community that has little international or ethnic diversity, you can gain some of the benefits of multicultural teams by seeking out people who work in different functional areas from yours. Or you can build a friendship with someone who has entirely different personal interests, political ideals, or religious beliefs. Thoughtfully interacting with individuals from these kinds of subcultures can also correlate with improving your overall CQ.[6]

A number of other relationships are being researched including the influence of gender, age, hometown, religious orientation, and profession on CQ; however, the research on these factors is still too incomplete to suggest any predictive relationships. While seeing the connection between these personal characteristics and experiences can be helpful, cultural intelligence is a dynamic set of abilities that can be nurtured and grown in all of us, regardless of our personality traits and experiences. Anyone can improve CQ, and the first step is understanding how one's background may influence the way one does so.

Results of Cultural Intelligence

What kind of results can you expect from enhancing your CQ? The research reveals promising outcomes for leaders with high CQ. This is one of the most important developments since the first edition of this book. The breadth and diversity of studies focused on the predictive results of high CQ has grown exponentially.[7] The following summarizes the most significant findings from the research. This comes back full circle to the global leadership challenges and opportunities examined in Chapter 1. Improved cultural intelligence helps you directly face the core issues facing today's global leaders.

Intercultural Adjustment

First, CQ is a consistent predictor of how you adapt in multicultural settings. Intercultural adjustment is the way a leader adjusts to the general living conditions of another culture. Your cultural intelligence is positively related to your ability to work and adapt to an environment where the assumptions, values, and traditions differ from those in your home context. In addition, CQ predicts how you will adapt to the work culture and the different ways of socializing in a new place. And CQ predicts your personal adjustment emotionally and psychologically when immersed in a new cultural environment.[8]

In particular, leaders with high CQ Drive and high CQ Action are better able to handle the psychological, emotional, and day-to-day adaptations they have to make in a new culture.[9] Extensive research based on findings from the *CQ Multi-Rater Assessment* (360°) reveals consistency between how a leader self-assesses CQ and how others rate his or her intercultural adjustment. Therefore, even a self-assessment of CQ reliably predicts how an individual will lead across cultures. And in reviewing the results of several thousand individuals who have taken the *CQ Multi-Rater Assessment*, a leader's observer ratings in CQ are consistently correlated with how that individual personally rates her CQ.[10]

Leaders who develop cultural intelligence are less likely to experience burnout from their intercultural work. Several studies reveal a connection between high CQ and a leader's level of stamina, energy, and productivity when working across borders. This finding is especially true for short-term business travelers who are expected to fly in and out of many different places from month to month.[11] Let's be honest. Even those of us who thrive on blazing the streets of a new place and trying the local food haunts eventually grow weary from having to continually adjust our approach to conflict resolution, negotiation, and casting vision for different cultural orientations. And jet lag and navigating different time zones can get to the best of us. But those leaders with higher CQ are better able to persevere through the inevitable stress and fatigue that result from this kind of cross-border work.

With higher CQ, you have a map and reference point to help interpret what's occurring. As a result, your ability to adjust internally and externally to the shifting expectations and demands of diverse cultures is enhanced through increased CQ. With higher CQ, you can better focus, do your job with excellence, and have a greater sense of fulfillment. And your CQ can improve your productivity while navigating intercultural situations and relationships.

Judgment and Decision Making

Another result of high CQ is improved ability to assess a situation in a culturally diverse situation and make an effective decision. The commonsense, lead-with-your-gut approach to making decisions doesn't cut it when leading outside your own cultural context. As noted in Chapter 1, the biggest challenge identified by today's senior-level executives is understanding customers across multiple locations in order to be able to make better decisions.[12] As overseas markets become more important, leaders across a wide range of organizations acknowledge a positive relationship between cultural intelligence and their ability to make informed decisions in light of the endless cultural differences. High CQ results in leaders who better diagnose situations and make effective decisions in culturally diverse contexts. Without the understanding offered by cultural intelligence, leaders are at a disadvantage for making strategic decisions both in their day-to-day operations and particularly in the midst of a crisis.[13]

No industry has felt the need for better judgment across intercultural situations more than the airlines. Since 9/11, airlines have become more acutely aware of the potential of having to handle a crisis. Pilots from two to three different cultural backgrounds commonly share the cockpit and flying responsibilities. International flights depend on communication between pilots and air traffic controllers across numerous countries. We all want these individuals to be able to effectively communicate and make good decisions. Airlines such as Lufthansa Airlines and Qatar Airways believe cultural intelligence plays a central part in their overall crisis management strategy and have integrated a plan for recruiting and developing culturally intelligent pilots.

Cultural intelligence has been found to predict judgment and better decision making from leaders who are working with intercultural issues and people (almost all of us!). In particular, there is a positive relationship between high CQ Knowledge and CQ Strategy and better intercultural judgment and decision making.[14]

Improved Negotiation

Negotiation is a critical component of any leader's job, which is why Chapter 7 used negotiation as an example of how to apply CQ Action. High CQ plays a significant role in improving a leader's likelihood of negotiating successfully across cultures—whether it's the formal negotiation of contracts or the day-to-day give-and-take required to reach agreements with staff, colleagues, vendors, and clients.

In particular, high CQ Drive provides leaders with the motivation to interact with their fellow negotiators, and a leader with higher CQ is more likely to present an appropriate negotiating posture to the other party. In addition, higher CQ Drive provides the negotiator with a much needed level of confidence to adapt to different negotiation practices and standards. Negotiating cross-culturally typically requires more time and a greater deal of patience to persist through the process.[15]

In addition, high CQ Strategy plays a significant role in a leader's effectiveness in negotiating across cultures. Developing an appropriate negotiation plan, being mindful and aware of what's going on in the midst of the negotiation, and following up to check for accuracy in one's interpretations are critical components of negotiating a deal that is not only agreeable but celebrated by everyone involved.[16]

Many Western organizations want a presence in places like China, and leaders with high CQ are more likely to effectively negotiate with Chinese officials and companies to make that happen. In China, companies are often asked to make changes or sacrifices for the greater interest of the nation. That's a foreign idea to many outsiders, particularly if the values of free enterprise and expression are the very things that seem to be at stake. But many Chinese insiders believe the high-pressure negotiation tactics used by Western leaders are the very things that erode their opportunities in China. Eva Cheng from Hong Kong, listed by *Forbes* as one of the one hundred most powerful women globally, says, "Google came close to putting its goal of cataloging the world's information in jeopardy by threatening to quit China when it discovered someone in the country was hacking the accounts of political dissidents."[17] If you decide to move into China with a new idea, you must fully convince the government why what you propose is good for the nation, the economy, and the Chinese people. Cheng says, "For the Chinese government, social stability overrides economic considerations. Politics come before economics. For business it is wiser to leave the fight over ideologies to the politicians and focus on the business agenda."[18] Our globally connected world requires that we negotiate across cultural borders on a daily basis. Higher CQ predicts we'll do so more successfully.

Leadership Performance

CQ also predicts the overall effectiveness of your leadership performance in culturally diverse situations. This includes leading a multicultural team to accomplish a shared goal and strategically managing an integrated enterprise across cultures. CQ Strategy and CQ Action are what most strongly predict your performance as a leader in intercultural contexts.[19] The research on performance-oriented outcomes related to high CQ is extensive, including the areas just discussed—judgment and decision making and negotiation—and it extends to other areas of performance such as effective communication, ideation, leadership development, and mergers and acquisitions.[20] There are a few specific areas of leadership performance worth examining as part of our discussion on the results of high CQ for you as a leader: technical proficiency, trust building, sales and service, and creativity and innovation.

TECHNICAL PROFICIENCY

In many twenty-first-century organizations, the most significant factor that determines who gets promoted to a leadership role is the individual's technical proficiency and track record in using that skill to produce results. For example, Bill McLawhon, head of leadership development at Facebook, told me,

> Leadership is not conferred based upon your position and title at Facebook. It comes naturally to individuals who have a high level of impact. Who are the individuals who create extraordinary value quickly? That kind of impact leads to followership, which confers leadership. The people who "ship it" and make an impact are the ones who are going to emerge as leaders.[21]

But because Facebook is a flat, meritocratic company, technical proficiency and results require an ability to influence and inspire people. And the more diversity among the people who need to be influenced and inspired, the greater the challenge of applying one's technical proficiency to a new context.

Leaders with higher levels of CQ are better able to bring their technical acumen with them into a new cultural context, whether that's scientific expertise, accounting, or public speaking.[22] Particularly as many organizations move toward a matrix, decentralized structure, one's ability to exert influence on peers and use one's technical proficiency in another cultural context becomes a distinguishing characteristic. High CQ is positively related to leadership emergence.[23]

TRUST BUILDING

Another critical capability that leads to effective, strategic leadership across cultures is the ability to build trusting intercultural relationships—with diverse colleagues; among multicultural teams; and with clients, vendors, and partners around the world. Trust means different things to different cultures and it's largely based on an intuitive interpretation of whether you believe another individual or organization is dependable. But that subjective interpretation of trust means everything. The very same behavior can elicit trust for one individual or culture and erode it in another. For example, a leader in a low power-distance culture might earn trust by sharing an example about when she failed, whereas doing that in a high power-distance culture, especially too early on with a group, might diminish trust and credibility.

Leaders with higher CQ are more likely to build trusting relationships with culturally diverse colleagues, clients, and constituents. In particular, high CQ Strategy emerges as a critical component of leaders who can effectively build trust across cultures.[24]

SALES AND SERVICE

Leaders with high CQ are better able to drive growth in new cultural markets and effectively serve diverse customers. Daniel Pink, in his book *To Sell Is Human*, states, "The purpose of the [sales] pitch isn't necessarily to move others immediately to adopt your idea. The purpose is to offer something so compelling that it begins as a conversation, brings the other person in as a participant, and eventually arrives at an outcome that appeals to both of you."[25] CQ will help you make a compelling pitch in a different cultural context because what a customer considers appealing and compelling is culturally bound.

The sales techniques required to be successful in China or India demand a high level of CQ. Doug Flint, CFO of banking giant HSBC, says:

> If you were to go into any business forum in Europe and America and ask which country is going to be most important in the global environment in the next 25 years, I suspect that a vast majority would say China, and the second-highest number might say India. If you then ask how much do people in Europe and America understand about the history and culture of those countries, the answer would be a negligible amount.[26]

Higher CQ will enhance your ability to understand what's compelling to people from different cultures. You will realize there's no such thing as a single market in China or the United States and you will be better able to sell your idea, services, or products to culturally diverse customers.[27]

CREATIVITY AND INNOVATION

Creativity and innovation are seen as essential strengths needed by those put in global leadership positions. A consistent correlation has been found between high CQ and ideation capabilities. However, this doesn't mean that all creative leaders are culturally intelligent leaders. We have daily examples of creative entertainers and executives who show very little cultural intelligence. But research does reveal a correlation in the other direction: Those with high CQ demonstrate a higher level of creativity than those with lower levels of CQ.[28] Improve your cultural intelligence and you'll also exercise your creativity muscle.

Think about the creativity that is often required of a leader who is working with a variety of cultures. You're trying to figure out how to get a team motivated to complete a particular task. If the team members come from a variety of cultural backgrounds, it's going to require some creativity for you to get everyone moving in the same direction. Or if you're trying to pitch the same idea to different cultural markets, creativity is often required. Therefore, as you grow your cultural intelligence, you're also growing your creativity.

A growing number of executives identify CQ as highly instrumental in offering them a competitive advantage for tapping into the opportunities of the twenty-first-century landscape. When individuals take the *CQ Multi-Rater Assessment*, they get personalized feedback on their progress toward the four results of CQ: intercultural adjustment, judgment and decision making, improved negotiation, and leadership performance.[29]

ROI for Organizations

What kind of ROI can organizations anticipate when cultural intelligence is enhanced? From the big picture, the most important ROI is that organizations with culturally intelligent leaders are more likely to accomplish their mission. Barclays, a mammoth financial services provider, utilized cultural intelligence with top leaders to deal with the company's burgeoning operations across Europe, Africa, Asia, Australia, the Americas, and the Middle East. As Barclays began to weave cultural intelligence throughout the top levels of the company, it experienced growth in the level of local ownership felt across its widespread global workforce. Previous attempts at restructuring and collaborating around a shared vision hadn't accomplished this, but when cultural intelligence became a priority among the top leadership there was a marked difference. Lloyds TSB took the challenge of improving customer relationships through cultural intelligence, which resulted in increased income streams and better cost management. And Levi Strauss has significantly altered its global marketing strategy as a result of cultural intelligence and simultaneously found a correlation in its profit margins.[30] Many other businesses, universities, charitable organizations, and governments have seen similar positive gains from using cultural intelligence to achieve their desired outcomes.

Given the results that consistently emerge for leaders with high CQ, there are several related outcomes for organizations that improve cultural intelligence. Most of these are simply the collective expression of the personal results we just covered, but it's worth noting the ROI of high CQ for teams and organizations. More research is needed to examine the long-term impact of improved cultural intelligence at the organizational level but the following are some of the initial findings.

Improved Multicultural Team Performance

All the dynamics and challenges that exist on any team are exacerbated when the team includes culturally diverse participants. And those challenges are even more pronounced if the team is globally dispersed and communicates primarily through email and conference calls. But when led well, a multicultural team offers an organization a tremendous resource for innovation and expanded opportunity. This begins with the leader of the team improving and applying cultural intelligence to how he facilitates the group. But it must also include developing the cultural intelligence of the team members, given that a team will be only as strong as its weakest member. Organizations that improve cultural intelligence see improved communication and performance among their diverse teams.[31]

Expansion into Culturally Diverse Markets (Global or Domestic)

Previously, I noted that a majority of executives surveyed are putting in a concerted effort toward international expansion because of the realization that their greatest opportunities for growth lay outside their domestic markets.[32] Companies such as NTT, a mammoth Japanese telecom, are aggressively expanding their presence in Africa and the Middle East. German companies such as Rocket Internet have grown by moving into markets such as Nigeria. Wal-Mart, Tesco, and Carrefour are bumping up against each other in the race to lure the emerging middle class in markets previously overlooked by these kinds of companies. And Larry Lieberman, owner of a small decorative lighting company in Long Island, New York, said sales to foreign markets, including Europe, China, and Japan, were the only thing that kept his business alive during the recession. He remarked, "If we only had domestic sales we would have been in big trouble in 2012."[33] These companies have utilized cultural intelligence to retain their corporate identities while adapting the ways they deliver their products and services based on what diverse markets require.

Imagine investing over one hundred million dollars in a new market only to have the government shut you down. That's exactly what happened to Amway, the direct-sales giant, when the Chinese government decided China wasn't ready for direct selling. Eva Cheng, executive vice president for Amway Asia at the time, had to decide how to advise her U.S. bosses and whether to invest additional effort and money in China. She drew on her cultural intelligence to figure out how to convince Amway to change its business strategy to align with the Chinese government's priorities while still remaining true to the non-negotiables of the privately owned U.S. company. The result? Not only did China change its policy on direct selling but the Asian arm of Amway began to shape the way Amway did business back home as well. Today, Amway Asia continues to be the largest revenue stream in the company's continually growing bottom line, far outpacing revenues from any other part of the world.

Meanwhile, Chinese organizations are looking for talent who can help them expand internationally. Chinese companies across numerous industries want to brand, sell, invest, acquire, and incorporate abroad, and culturally intelligent leaders are in a position to support and lead these efforts.

One of the best examples of a Chinese company that has used the benefits of high CQ to expand internationally is the Dalian Wanda Group, a conglomerate in the real estate, tourism, and entertainment business. After they acquired AMC Entertainment Holdings, they identified and recruited talent who had the ability to work effectively in different cultures (CQ) as well as seeking individuals with language proficiency for the target markets, including English, Spanish, and Russian. And when China's Suanghui recently acquired Smithfield Foods for $4.7 billion, it looked for bilingual, culturally intelligent executives to help the company manage its relationship with the United States' largest pork producer.[34]

One survey found that 45 percent of Chinese business leaders surveyed considered cultural challenges to be one of the biggest barriers to successfully acquiring or partnering with Western businesses. As a result, a growing number of Chinese companies are putting greater emphasis on hiring culturally intelligent talent.[35] One Chinese sector that has already done a remarkable job of integrating international talent is the technology industry. Companies such as Baidu, Alibaba, and Lenovo have a track record of successfully recruiting top foreign graduates into their ranks to support their international communications, operations, and research and development work. We'll look further at the kinds of best practices used by organizations that have done this successfully in the next chapter.

Better Service to Culturally Diverse Customers, Patients, or Students

In the age of instant posts and photos, it's never been more important for organizations to provide good service to constituents, regardless of their cultural background. Organizations with leaders and team members who have higher CQ are better able to anticipate the best way to serve culturally diverse customers, and when mistakes occur, they have a better idea of the appropriate way to respond. Media company IAC was wise to immediately fire PR executive Justine Sacco when she tweeted, "Going to Africa. Hope I don't get AIDS. Just kidding. I'm White!" But one has to wonder what kind of PR work she had been doing on behalf of the company prior to this gaffe. I have plenty of grace for stupid comments. We all make them. But it seems that even a moderate level of CQ would cause someone to self-filter before posting the kind of statement made by Sacco. As you invest in developing the cultural intelligence of your team, the return will easily come back in the trust and reputation it garners for you with your constituents.

Speed and Efficiency

Most businesses, government agencies, and nonprofit organizations are trying to do more with less. When led by leaders with high CQ, organizations are able to accomplish results in culturally diverse contexts more quickly. They close deals more quickly than organizations with leaders who have low CQ. Keep in mind that "more quickly" is relative and deals almost always take longer when they involve different cultures. But when cultural intelligence is raised, organizations can better adjust their timelines and expectations based on the cultural value orientations involved. Timely delivery and follow-through are more likely in organizations with leaders who have higher CQ.

Productive Global Assignments

Sending personnel overseas is costly and the whole pursuit has often had a fifty-fifty chance when it comes to whether the expat will complete the assignment much less be productive. Global assignments are much more likely to be effective when CQ is higher and better yet if the expat's partner and children have high CQ Drive. Leaders who have higher CQ are more successful at completing assignments because they learn faster and are better equipped to persevere through the culture shock and frustration that often ensues. In addition, organizations that assess and develop CQ in their leaders who move overseas are more likely to create a plan for the leader's reentry after the assignment, including finding ways to learn from the leader's overseas experience.[36]

Employer of Choice

As noted previously, attracting and retaining good talent is another pressing need felt by leading executives.[37] A company's chances of being the employer of choice is enhanced when recruits see cultural intelligence valued and modeled throughout the organization as a whole. Companies such as Novartis and Nike discovered that their sharpest recruits identified a culturally intelligent environment and reputation as one of the most important things they sought in a potential employer. They wanted to join companies that see diversity as a leading growth edge for business rather than as a roadblock or a necessary evil.

Eighty-five percent of emerging leaders strongly agree that global sensibilities and a commitment to the common good are extremely important to them in thinking about a current or future employer. They want places of employment where they can grow and develop in CQ by seeing it modeled and prioritized.[38]

Profitability and Cost Savings

What about the almighty bottom line? There is research that indicates a correlation between improved CQ and profitability and cost savings. But the most compelling evidence for this correlation stems from all the previous results discussed. If an organization succeeds at improving team performance, expanding into and serving new markets, improving efficiency, increasing effectiveness in global assignments, and decreasing turnover, it's pretty clear cultural intelligence can have a direct impact on the bottom line.[39]

Much more research is needed to further expand our understanding of the results in store for culturally intelligent leaders and their organizations. But the initial results are extremely promising.

Conclusion

Simon, the former college president, is thriving in his new role leading the turnaround efforts at the consulting firm. He has a globally dispersed team of trainers and coaches across fifteen countries, and the company just had its best year of financial gains. I'd be the first to acknowledge that numerous factors have contributed to Simon's success. But a survey of his personnel revealed the main factor is that Simon possesses an unusual ability to offer a compelling, unifying vision across the company while allowing each unit to contextualize its work as it sees best. It's hard to believe this is the same leader I heard described as "inauthentic and manipulative" by his New England colleagues.

Cultural intelligence is directly tied to personal and organizational performance. A number of factors shape an individual's CQ but everyone can grow in the journey toward leading across borders effectively. That leads us to the final chapter: "Developing a Culturally Intelligent Team."

CHAPTER 9

DEVELOPING A CULTURALLY INTELLIGENT TEAM

Most of the book has focused on how to personally develop and apply your cultural intelligence as a leader. But as we discover the personal benefits of cultural intelligence, we inevitably want to develop it in those we lead. This final chapter covers the strategies for developing a culturally intelligent organization or team.

Assessing and developing cultural intelligence at the organizational level is one of the emerging frontiers in the cultural intelligence research. Much more research is needed to better understand what it looks like to create a culturally intelligent organization. But universities, companies, and NGOs around the world are using the following best practices for developing more culturally intelligent teams, divisions, and overall organizations. These practices can be scaled to teams or to an entire organization.

Leadership Commitment

Unless senior leaders embody the values and vision of your organization, those ideas remain mere words on a PowerPoint presentation or web page. This is especially true when embracing a vision for becoming a more culturally intelligent force in the world. The level of CQ among senior leaders is the most consistent variable linked to whether or not an organization functions in the world with a track record of dignity, respect, and social responsibility. Senior leaders have to prioritize cultural intelligence in order to see it become a guiding characteristic and modus operandi throughout the organization as a whole. Coping with and responding to fast-changing circumstances and the enactment of a global strategy rests on a team of senior leaders who can draw on the four capabilities of cultural intelligence.[1]

Begin by painting a picture for your leaders of what it looks like to become a more culturally intelligent organization. Questions I consistently use when interacting with executives about this include the following:

- What are your key performance goals and targets?
- What are the biggest challenges hindering you from reaching those goals?
- In what way does culture play a part in these challenges (e.g., a dispersed workforce, multicultural teams, culturally diverse markets, expatriate assignments, short-term travel, retaining core values)?
- In what way could improved cultural intelligence help your team overcome your challenges and accomplish your goals (e.g., better insights into diverse customers, improved employee engagement, innovative opportunities, faster to market)?

Leadership commitment is demonstrated by integrating cultural intelligence with accomplishing your overall mission rather than addressing cultural intelligence as an end in itself or isolating it as only relevant to those doing international work. The truly global organization will integrate cultural intelligence across all functions and as part of the strategic plan.

For example, how does cultural intelligence influence the way an organization pursues research and development? Several years ago, Steelcase, one of the world's leaders in the office furniture industry, decided to take advantage of the opportunity to expand into Japan. The Japanese expressed a high level of interest in and recognized a potential demand for Steelcase's new line of desks and chairs. Steelcase promptly shipped two containers full of the furniture to Japan, rented prime space in downtown Tokyo for a display room, and then watched the furniture sit on display with very limited sales. Many people would come in and try sitting at the desks but very few sold. Much later, Steelcase discovered that the chairs, which were designed for larger North Americans, were uncomfortable for the smaller-framed Japanese. And the large desks symbolized a pretense unwanted by Japanese executives. The company shipped all the furniture back home and worked with Japanese engineers to redesign the product specifically with Asian customers in mind. Five years later, Steelcase was the largest office furniture distributor in Asia.

Toyota learned a similar lesson going the other direction across the ocean. For many years, Toyota struggled to compete with Honda and Chrysler in the North American minivan market. So it decided to redesign its minivan, the Sienna. Yuji Yokoya was tasked with the job. He started the R&D process by driving the current Toyota minivan through every U.S. state, all thirteen Canadian provinces and territories, and all across Mexico. His on-the-ground experiences in North America gave him insights that would have been entirely missed if he had simply researched market trends and North American demographics from an office in Japan. For example, he discovered that many Canadian highways have a higher crown than Japanese roads—bowed in the middle, presumably to deal with snow. That led him to see the importance of a design that dealt with the inevitable drift that happened as the van travelled along the sloped road.

One of the biggest differences between Japanese and North American cultures is the way people eat. Japanese rarely eat on the go. If a Japanese family is driving and gets thirsty or hungry, they're most likely to stop to consume a snack or drink before getting back in the van. But North Americans take their food and beverages with them, often packing or purchasing snacks along the way and filling up large drink containers to bring in the van. In fact, Yokoya learned that many U.S. drivers want at least two drinking compartments for each passenger. The result of his finding was the installation of fourteen cup and bottle holders in the newly designed Sienna as well as a flip-up tray for food.[2]

This is what it looks like to integrate cultural intelligence with R&D. And the same can be said for how cultural intelligence can be applied to manufacturing, as well as the human resources, legal, and sales departments. If a German company is developing a production timeline that assumes it can reach a contract with a subsidiary in China in time to meet a deadline, the manufacturing leaders are going to need cultural intelligence to determine how to negotiate in a way that will appeal to the values of Chinese business. When a Chinese company is developing a cross-border agreement with a Nigerian company, it needs to identify the key competitive factors associated with working together, assess the cultural and organizational risks connected with each of those factors, and draw on this information in its corporate decision making.[3] And university leaders that draw large populations of international students need to consider how admissions officers, faculty, and student development staff are equipped to meet the different values, assumptions, and behaviors of a culturally diverse student body while still following a standard of expectations for the entire campus community.

One of the challenges for leaders who are developing a culturally intelligent organization is developing malleable structures that accommodate cultural differences while not reinventing the entire system for every cultural context. Customizing and adapting structures is essential but it's unsustainable to build a completely new structure and delivery system for each situation. A coherent approach that is both standardized and malleable ultimately rests on organizational leaders who embody the ethos of the organization and who are committed to pursuing the mission in a culturally intelligent way.

Assessment

The oft-quoted mantra "You are what you measure" applies here, as does "What gets measured counts." The majority of K–12 (primary and secondary) schools I enter around the world post a mission statement about preparing global citizens. And many of them list cultural competency as a core learning outcome. But when administrators are asked how they're evaluating students' development as culturally competent global citizens, there's usually very little substance to the response. It's much more varied when you ask that question of corporate, hospital, or NGO organizations. Some are very intentional about assessing the development of culturally intelligent personnel and others are not. It's difficult, if not impossible, to develop a culturally intelligent team unless some measurement is involved. Keep in mind that cultural intelligence is something any individual or organization can improve, so assessment is not something to be feared or resisted. Instead, it allows a reality check to see where the team is against a benchmark of where you want it to be.

You can begin by doing an audit of your team or organization as a whole. To what degree do the practices, policies, and marketing messages of the organization reflect a culturally intelligent approach? What cultures are represented in the organization? What cultures are underrepresented? The audit can also include a qualitative assessment of the cultural intelligence of your team. To what degree do the leaders value, demonstrate, and promote culturally intelligent behavior? How are we hiring and promoting with a consideration of one's CQ? To what degree do we have diverse representation from various cultures on our teams and how have we equipped teams to engage with that diversity? What would our constituents say about our level of cultural intelligence? And you can qualitatively assess individual personnel using the model we've walked through in the book:

1. CQ Drive: What's this individual's motivation for intercultural work and relationships?

2. CQ Knowledge: To what degree does this individual understand core cultural differences?

3. CQ Strategy: How well does this individual plan for culturally diverse situations?

4. CQ Action: To what degree does this individual appropriately adapt for different cultural contexts?

Assessment may also include the use of quantitative measurements. The two key questions you should always consider before using any kind of quantitative survey, scorecard, or inventory are:

1. What do we want to measure?

2. What valid, reliable tools exist to measure this?

I'm amazed at how many times organizations use a tool to measure something other than what it's intended to measure. You don't use a ruler to determine the temperature outside. Yet some organizations assess global capabilities with a tool that was designed to measure something else, such as personal preferences or value orientations. Knowing one's personal value orientations (e.g., whether one prefers hierarchical structures or flat ones) is an essential aspect of self-awareness. If that's your primary goal, find a tool designed to measure that, such as GlobeSmart, Cultural Orientations Indicator, or CultureWizard. But if you want to assess someone's skills for working across cultures, you need a different kind of assessment. This was the need that drove us to develop the CQ assessments. We had reviewed and benefited from other inventories that were more focused on one's attitude toward different cultures or personality traits—valuable insights, but something different from what we wanted to measure. Our interest was in seeing whether you could assess and predict intercultural *performance* combined with personal value orientations.

In looking at whether a tool is academically reliable and valid, investigate this as you would anything else. If a hotel tells you it's the best hotel in a city, you're probably more interested in what hospitality critics and guests say about the hotel than the hotel itself. Most assessments are described as academically valid and reliable, but the important question is, Were the items made available to external academics who experienced consistent results using the instrument? The CQ Scale has been vetted, reviewed, and validated by academics from all over the world who had no personal, vested interest in CQ.

There are a variety of ways to effectively assess your team's progress toward becoming more culturally intelligent. The key point is to determine how you will measure this in your organization.

Learning and Development

The most typical way organizations develop culturally intelligent teams is through learning and development initiatives. Although training shouldn't be the only method used to implement CQ, it is an important facet. Effectively learning about cultural intelligence begins with addressing CQ Drive. Mandating that employees sit through training on diversity or cross-border negotiation doesn't ensure an interested, engaged group of participants. For those of us who step into learning situations in which people are required to participate, we have to make a convincing case for why individuals should care about cultural intelligence. Connections need to be made between cultural intelligence and their personal interests. Here are a few suggestions for educating teams about cultural intelligence:

Show-and-Tell

Gather your team and explain the benefits of cultural intelligence to them personally and to the organization as a whole. Communicate the corresponding costs for cultural ignorance. Use the research findings from Chapter 8 to demonstrate the payoffs of cultural intelligence. Talk about the connection between cultural intelligence and organizational goals rather than just about cultural intelligence as an end in itself. In so doing, you'll tap into the cultural intelligence Drive element before immediately jumping into the other issues of cultural intelligence. Teach the four CQ capabilities as a model to use in any intercultural situation. Begin to interest your team in how cultural intelligence can help them enhance careers and prevent becoming vocationally obsolete.

Functional Training

Once you go beyond the typical ninety-minute introduction to cultural intelligence, most teams will need and want training that is specifically focused on how to apply cultural intelligence to their particular functions. The sales team needs to see how cultural intelligence will help them pitch and sell more effectively, and the R&D team needs to see how improved CQ will enhance their research and innovations. The same is true for marketing personnel who need to understand how cultural intelligence will help them effectively market to a culture that is more cooperatively oriented versus one that is more competitively oriented (see Chapter 5). Clearly, there are times when cross-functional training is valuable to avoid perpetuating the silo effect. But I find most teams grow frustrated when cultural intelligence is simply taught as an overarching, generic concept rather than having its application cutomized to specific roles and functions in the organization. Senior leaders usually can handle broader discussions about cultural intelligence from the big-picture view. But those working in functional units typically prefer to have concepts like cultural intelligence directly applied to their work in very concrete terms. Put primary energy into offering functional expertise on the application of cultural intelligence to different departments and functions in your organization and develop case studies, discussions, and exercises that directly apply to them.

Personal CQ Development Plan

Include cultural intelligence as an area for team members to consider when completing their annual development plan. Offer coaching on ways they can enhance their CQ based on the kinds of strategies shared throughout this book. The more the plan aligns with their personal motivation and interests, the better. Ask them to identify one objective for each of the four capabilities—measurable steps to grow their CQ Drive, Knowledge, Strategy, and Action. Or have them identify one of the four capabilities that most needs attention this year.

Many organizations are also including cultural intelligence as a part of the annual performance review—not so much as an evaluative dimension but more as a developmental area to revisit each year. Many of these organizations encourage personnel to choose from a variety of online or face-to-face courses on topics such as culturally intelligent negotiation, effective virtual teams, or country-specific offerings. Resources are available to help individuals learn new ways of seeing and doing things in a variety of contexts.[4]

The most important way to nurture and develop cultural intelligence throughout the organization is by personally modeling it. Demonstrate a high value for the strategic benefits of cultural intelligence to you as a leader, to the organization, and to the greater good of humanity. Describe the relevance of the four CQ capabilities to something you're doing. And model the value of learning from mistakes. In fact, the culturally intelligent leader is someone who has learned to use her mistakes as a source of inspiration for change. When encountering a new culture, you will inevitably experience a few failures and setbacks. The critical issue is not flawless behavior but how you learn from your mistakes and negative experiences. High CQ helps you pay attention to what you can learn from both good and bad experiences cross-culturally.[5]

Nurture a community of lifelong learners to work and live in our multicultural world. Find creative ways to inspire and educate your team to grow in cultural intelligence. Give lots of encouragement and empower your team to take ownership of some of your emerging initiatives in new cultural markets.[6] Guide them through the process and help them apply cultural intelligence to the assignment. As you do so, you'll give them a skill set that will allow them to tap into the unprecedented opportunities of the twenty-first-century world. And your organization will have a decided edge for staying ahead of the curve.

Hiring and Promotion

In many ways, your organization is whomever someone encounters on the other end of an email or phone call. While individuals in senior positions of leadership are the ones who have to lead the way in embracing and prioritizing cultural intelligence, eventually most of the personnel throughout an organization need some measure of cultural intelligence. The greater the degree and amount of cultural distance encountered by team members in their daily work, the more important it is for them to understand and grow in cultural intelligence. Therefore, the most obvious positions where cultural intelligence should become a required skill set among your team include international project managers, individuals fulfilling expatriate assignments, and representatives who are expected to travel internationally on your behalf.

But consider how to develop cultural intelligence even among personnel who don't fill the kinds of positions that have direct responsibility for negotiating and working cross-culturally. The support person answering emails and returning phone calls *is* your organization to the individual on the other end of that email or phone call. The faculty member teaching students behind closed doors in the classroom *is* your university to those students. The nurse treating the immigrant *is* your hospital to that patient and his family. Reflecting cultural intelligence in the way you write your mission statement, market your products, or share your vision is important. But it pales in contrast with the role your personnel play in communicating how your organization functions among people of difference. The way your team behaves cross-culturally reflects on your entire organization as well as on them personally. Begin by assessing the degree to which cultural intelligence is important for various functions in the organization, with two of the most important being human resources professionals and those who travel internationally.

Human Resources

There are few departments for which cultural intelligence has as much direct relevance to its day-to-day work as the human resources department. Don't hire an HR director who doesn't have high CQ! HR directors need high CQ to analyze and fill various jobs within the organization and to drive recruitment, performance reviews, training, and career planning.[7] The four-capability model of cultural intelligence offers HR directors a consistent model for everything from promoting respect among a diverse workforce to creating policies that attend to religious and cultural diversity among personnel. HR professionals need cultural intelligence to develop it in others and for screening, recruiting, and developing individuals for work assignments that include international travel.

International Travelers

Individuals who travel on behalf of the organization need high CQ more than those who stay home. Project managers who are in daily contact with suppliers and customers in international markets will often need to travel to unfamiliar cultures. And cultural intelligence is needed most by staff deployed for extended overseas assignments. Don't just recruit individuals with the technical competence for the job; they should also have stronger CQ than individuals who fill the same kind of positions at home. Pay attention to team members and candidates who demonstrate a high level of self-efficacy for international assignments. Assess their CQ and carefully consider whether to eliminate candidates with low CQ Drive or find ways to help them develop and grow. Your decision can save you thousands and sometimes millions of dollars. Don't miss this! Just because someone is a great engineer in Atlanta doesn't mean that person will perform well as an engineer in Dubai.

After carefully selecting an individual for an international assignment, offer that person ongoing training and development. Don't just do pre-departure training. Clearly some information and awareness are needed on the front end. The emphasis in pre-departure orientation should be on learning how to survive during the first six months and learning what questions to ask. But there's often a much higher level of motivation for learning about CQ midway through an international assignment rather than at the beginning. Too much pre-departure training can feel irrelevant and theoretical to the individual who is mostly trying to figure out how to pack up her home and move to the other side of the world. But after being engaged in a foreign assignment for a while, a whole new set of questions emerges along with a pent-up desire to find solutions to working and living overseas. This is a far better time to offer more thorough training in cultural intelligence than inoculating employees with too much at the front end.

Screen Candidates for CQ

In looking for culturally intelligent personnel to fill the roles of HR directors and international travelers, assess them in the four CQ capabilities. In addition to using a CQ assessment, ask questions such as the following when interviewing, observing, and checking references:

CQ DRIVE

- ☐ To what degree does she show an interest in different cultures?
- ☐ Has she sought out opportunities to work with colleagues from different backgrounds?
- ☐ What's her confidence level like when engaging in cross-cultural situations?

CQ KNOWLEDGE

- ☐ How does he demonstrate insight into how culture influences his decision making?
- ☐ Can he describe the basic cultural differences that exist among the cultures where the organization works?
- ☐ Does he speak another language? Can he read in between the lines of what someone is saying?

CQ STRATEGY

- ☐ How does she demonstrate awareness of herself and others?
- ☐ How does she plan differently for cross-cultural interactions and work?
- ☐ Does she check back to see if her cross-cultural behavior is effective?

CQ ACTION

- ☐ Can he alter his communication for various contexts?
- ☐ Does he demonstrate flexible negotiation skills?
- ☐ To what degree does he flex his behavior when working with people and projects in different cultural contexts?

Reward Culturally Intelligent Performance

Celebrate the diversity across your organization and reward culturally intelligent behavior. Keep in mind the cultural and individual differences for what motivates various team members. For some, financial remuneration is the most compelling incentive, whereas for others it might be job fulfillment, job security, flextime, or status. Challenge your team to embrace a transcendent motivation for treating people with dignity and respect and for making the world a better place. Give them a vision for being a community of individuals who are committed to the greater good and to being an agent for respectful and humane global engagement. Here's something you might consider: Growing numbers of organizations are giving employees one week of paid time to do volunteer tourism somewhere in the world. They realize the payoff that comes from having employees travel to another part of the world and the ways it allows the organization to contribute to something bigger than itself. In return, employees tap into one of the greatest tools for becoming more culturally intelligent: international travel.[8] One Los Angeles–based manufacturing company has created a foundation wherein the company helps provide clean water filters for several communities throughout Sub-Saharan Africa. It also offers employees one week of paid time to do volunteer service in one of these regions. And employees can even apply for grant money from the company's foundation to help fund their trips. The CEO and employees both find great return on this investment.

Determine the areas where it's most important to have culturally intelligent personnel and work with your HR department to ensure those positions are filled with culturally intelligent individuals. The cost of senior leadership's time and lost opportunities from not doing so is too great. Join the organizations on the front edge of leading in a diverse world that see cultural intelligence as a driving priority for personnel.

Branding

So how do you integrate cultural intelligence with your overall mission and value proposition? Permeate your strategic plan with action steps that move you toward more culturally intelligent behavior in every department. Instead of being stretched and overrun by globalization and virtual work teams, tap into the strengths and opportunities that exist within these diverse perspectives and locations. And develop a reputation for being a twenty-first-century organization that reflects cultural intelligence in your people, products, marketing, and service. Make it part of your core values and include it as part of your brand statement.

Imagine being an organization that not only survives in the unpredictable, chaotic world of globalization but actually thrives in it. Develop a vision for defying the abysmal statistics that predict a 70 percent failure rate among all international ventures. And believe that culturally intelligent leaders and organizations enjoy tangible and altruistic profits that far outweigh the costs. The research cited throughout this book has proven again and again the economic value added by integrating cultural intelligence into your leadership role and into your organization. Join a movement of leaders who are making cultural intelligence the modus operandi for twenty-first-century leadership by making it central to your mission, vision, and values.

Create Third-Space Strategies

The question many leaders ask is "Who adapts to whom?" If a Chinese executive is meeting with a colleague from Germany, should the meeting follow Chinese protocol or German? Or if you're opening an office in a new market, how much should you localize and how much of your value proposition are the things you've succeeded at elsewhere?

McDonald's fries and shakes taste pretty similar in Chicago and Delhi. There's some uniformity to the experience of eating at McDonald's most anywhere. But the localized approaches to menus demonstrate flexible structures within McDonald's international approach. The flavors of shakes available in Chicago and Delhi restaurants are different. And the basic McDonald's product, the hamburger, isn't available at Indian restaurants. McDonald's has developed a third-space approach that adapts to Hindu convictions toward cows. So instead of the Big Mac, the McVeggie is at the center of the McDonald's menu in India. Flexible structures, services, and products are what help your team and organization find a third space that works for you.

For most leaders and teams, insisting that everyone adapt to "headquarters" doesn't cut it anymore. But neither is it realistic to think an organization can fully localize. Conventional wisdom therefore usually follows the Venn diagram approach: Find the areas where you have common ground and work from there. That's not a bad starting point, but there are several limitations including the risk that you will lose the value of the distinctions each culture brings (by focusing too much on what you have in common), and in some situations, very little common ground may exist aside from a shared objective of making money or seeing an objective accomplished.

Instead, rather than simply finding the intersection of individual goals or insisting on one or the other side doing all the adjusting, a culturally intelligent team will create a third, alternative space in which to work and relate together. This doesn't mean that each individual, unit, or culture is fully stripped of its distinctive values and contributions. That would rob teams of one of the greatest benefits of diverse perspectives. But it does mean that there's an intentional attempt to develop an alternative culture together and benefit from the fusion that results. This is an area where my colleagues and I are currently focusing our research and writing, and it's the topic of my next book: What are the routines for how an organization creates and implements a third space? And how can those third-space strategies be used to drive innovation and better solutions? The idea is to identify and use a set of research-based routines throughout the organization to enable it to function day to day in culturally intelligent ways.

Beware. The tendency is for the dominant culture to presume its way is the transcultural gold standard that works best for everyone. Creating an alternative space thus requires a great deal of effort and deliberation and is often best facilitated by an external change management facilitator who has a high level of CQ and can help you reach that third space.

Conclusion

With every passing year, the importance of leading with cultural intelligence becomes increasingly significant. You can have all the right policies and make all the right tactical decisions, but if you don't engage with cultural intelligence, forget it! Accomplishing your performance objectives will be a crapshoot at best and you have a 70 percent chance of failure.

Many organizational leaders pursue international growth and diversity. But by failing to consciously develop a strategy for becoming a culturally intelligent organization, most of these pursuits fall short. By tapping into the research surrounding cultural intelligence, you and your organization need not become one more statistic of failure in working across borders. Cultural intelligence offers a pathway forward. It's a proven way of enhancing your personal leadership capabilities and it provides a framework for designing a more effective global organization. And while you're at it, by leading with cultural intelligence, you can make a world of difference near and far.

EPILOGUE

CAN YOU REALLY BE A GLOBAL LEADER?

All of us have unspoken assumptions about what makes a good leader. Many of these stem from our cultural backgrounds. And as with any cultural bias, oftentimes we're not even aware of our leadership assumptions.

For example, what if you interview someone for a leadership position and that person isn't tall? Most of us would say that's irrelevant. But we've heard again and again that if you want to be a CEO in the United States, it sure helps if you're tall. The average height of U.S. males is five feet, nine inches and only 14 percent are six feet or taller. Yet, 58 percent of CEOs in the United States are six feet or taller.

In Mexico, people expect their leaders to have a benevolent relationship with those they manage, somewhat akin to what we might expect among parents and children. However, leading with that kind of style in many European contexts would be deemed patronizing and off-putting. And many African employees expect their leaders to display chieflike behaviors in how they manage the company, something that would be leadership suicide in many other contexts.

As I've noted repeatedly, your ability to lead has as much to do with the expectations and stereotypes of your followers as it does your behavior as a leader. Just recall Simon's experience at a New England college compared to the other organizations where he led. This sounds daunting for those of us aspiring to lead in a world that's getting flatter and smaller. And most of us have to manage people from lots of different cultural backgrounds. But with improved CQ, it is possible to be an effective global leader who not only survives but also thrives!

Cultural intelligence is an important skill set for anyone living and working in the twenty-first-century world but it's essential for leaders in order to *lead*. Profitable and sustainable businesses need executives who understand diverse markets. Successful military missions depend on officers who can lead their personnel to engage strategically. Charitable causes need globally minded leaders who can work across national borders effectively. If leaders don't become culturally intelligent, they'll be managed by the cultures where they work rather than leading by their guiding values and objectives.[1] Your CQ can improve. It's something anyone can develop and learn, assuming the individual has the interest to do so.

Here are a few parting words as you continue the quest of leading with cultural intelligence:

1. *Get rid of one-size-fits-all leadership mantras.* Talking about "irrefutable laws of leadership" makes for nice seminar material but it doesn't work so great when working globally. For example, using an "empowering style of leadership" is usually lauded as an essential approach for any leader. And it's certainly a style that I prefer personally. But I work with many individuals in high power-distance cultures for whom it's very disorienting to feel like their manager isn't being directive with them about what needs to be done. On the other hand, a leader who uses a very prescriptive and directive approach with someone who prefers a more empowering approach is going to hit the wall.

2. *Consciously adapt your leadership style according to the situation and followers.* Many of us have people from different cultures working on the same team, so we have to figure out how this can be done in a way that doesn't become discriminatory or unrealistic. This is where cultural intel-

ligence comes in—the capability to adapt to different cultures in order to motivate people to accomplish a shared set of objectives.

3. *Leading with cultural intelligence doesn't mean being a chameleon to suit every individual and situation encountered.* But it does mean knowing when an empowering style is most necessary compared to a more directive one. The same applies to when we should address conflict head-on, and when we need to be more indirect (yes, both are appropriate!). And as we grow in the four capabilities of cultural intelligence, we increasingly know how to adapt on the fly to various situations that arise.

4. *Be yourself . . . but creatively.* While culturally intelligent leaders know how to adapt to various situations and followers, they also demonstrate a level of comfort in their own skin. Whether it's the company brand or one's personal identity, the challenge is how to adapt enough to accomplish our objectives in a way that's both respectful and effective but not go so far that we're no longer true to ourselves. Be yourself, but that may mean new and creative manifestations of how you express yourself as a leader.

ACKNOWLEDGMENTS

I'm incredibly grateful to Soon Ang and Linn Van Dyne, who began as professional colleagues and have long since become the dearest of friends. They inspired me to write the first edition of the book and generously shared their research, insights, critiques, and encouragement. They did the same for the second edition, and we continue to work together to advance the scholarship and application of cultural intelligence across the globe.

Second, this edition is an improvement over the first because of so many conversations and emails with readers and reviews of the first edition—both positive and a few not so positive. The input provoked me to think deeper about many of the ways cultural intelligence plays out for global leaders as well as about much needed adjustments and updates to keep this information relevant.

And as I worked on this second edition, I was reminded of the extensive, constructive input I received from the researchers and executives who read an early draft of the first edition: Soon Ang, Dick DeVos, Rebecca Kuiper, Linda Fenty, Don Maine, Kok Yee Ng, Sandra Upton, Linn Van Dyne, and Mike Volkema. Their experiences and perspectives profoundly shaped the book and I continued to hear their voices even while writing the revised edition.

When Christina Parisi from AMACOM invited me to write the first book, she started her email with "Ever since I went abroad in college, I've had an interest in this topic." It was deeply gratifying to shape the first edition with her editorial guidance. And it's been equally rewarding to work with Stephen S. Power, my new editor at AMACOM, who guided me through the revision process and affirmed the value of taking this edition to the next level.

My oldest daughter, Emily, has grown up to be a culturally intelligent young woman who will take CQ places I never imagined.

And my daughter Grace shares my love for adventure, discovering new places, and using cultural intelligence to make the world a better place. Finally, to be married to your best friend is a gift like none other. Linda lives out cultural intelligence in ways that far outshine me. And she forever gives me a safe place to return, regardless of how my ideas are accepted by others.

TEN CULTURAL CLUSTERS

I've compiled the norms for the cultural values of the ten largest cultural clusters in the world. These are what appear in the cultural value dimension tables in Chapter 5. Each of these clusters has similar patterns of thinking and behavior. All of the typical cautions about stereotyping apply here. You can't fully categorize the entire world into ten large groups, but these provide a good starting point for seeing one's self in light of the dominant norms. The countries listed with each cluster are examples of where large populations of that cluster can be found. But as diversity increases everywhere, most every country has people from multiple clusters. The ten clusters, based on the work of Ronen and Shenkar,[1] are as follows:

ANGLO: Found in places like Australia, Canada, New Zealand, United Kingdom, United States

Anglo cultures originated primarily in places where wide-open land was the norm, so people settled with a great deal of room between them and their neighbors. Most Anglos like their space. A ruthless, independent spirit strongly characterizes the majority of people in the Anglo cluster. The Anglo cluster is the most geographically dispersed of the ten cultural clusters. But what unites the Anglo cluster most is a shared ethnic and linguistic history: Caucasians who speak English. The cluster accounts for roughly 7 percent of the world yet it represents 40 percent of the world's gross domestic product.

ARAB: Found in places like Bahrain, Egypt, Jordan, Kuwait, Lebanon, Morocco, Saudi Arabia, United Arab Emirates

To be an Arab is a cultural identity more than an ethnic heritage. A key factor in identifying as an Arab is speaking Arabic as one's first language. Being an Arab also typically means having family ties that originate in this region, with the utmost value placed on honoring one's family. Being Arab doesn't necessarily mean one is a Muslim, but Islam has a ubiquitous influence on the cluster. Even those Arabs who aren't religiously devoted are usually influenced by some of the Islamic ideals and tenets, and they often refer to themselves as "cultural Muslims."

CONFUCIAN ASIA: Found in places like China, Hong Kong, Japan, Singapore, South Korea, Taiwan

Confucianism is sometimes called "the religion of *li*," because *li* is an integral part of the Confucian way of thinking and behaving. *Li* literally means "to arrange in order." *Li* means etiquette, customs, and manners; it's ceremony, courtesy, civility, and behaving with propriety. *Li* and the associated value of *ren* (benevolence) are organized around five key relationships that govern most of life in this cluster: ruler to subject, father to son, husband to wife, elder brother to younger brother, and elder friend to junior friend. When working with someone from Confucian Asia, determine which side of the relationship you're on.

EASTERN EUROPE: Found in places like Albania, Czech Republic, Greece, Hungary, Mongolia, Poland, Russia

The Eastern Europe cluster is perhaps the most diverse cluster of the ten, largely because it's a vast region with a long, relentless history of colonization. Sometimes the colonizing forces came from outside regions, whereas other times colonization was led by various groups within the cluster. The long-term impact of these varied colonizers can be seen through the diverse religions, customs, and languages. Many of the countries in this cluster have experienced significant geopolitical changes even in the last couple of decades. Eastern Europeans are increasingly identified as "Europeans" and will not appreciate being identified most as people from the "former Soviet republics."

GERMANIC EUROPE: Found in places like Austria, Belgium, Germany, Netherlands

The Germanic cluster has a long, rich heritage that goes back thousands of years. Germanic Europe is a relatively tight culture that is slow to change. The cluster is comparatively small, but it has a sizable economic footprint in the world, and countries in this cluster have deep economic ties with each another. The Germanic cluster has also been a leader in developing culture through its many renowned poets, novelists, musicians, and philosophers. Germanic cultures are widely known for making things happen and for placing a high priority on the rights of individuals.

LATIN AMERICA: Found in places like Argentina, Bolivia, Brazil, Chile, Columbia, Costa Rica, Mexico

The Latin America cluster shares a great deal with Latin Europe while also reflecting many of the indigenous cultures from Central and South America. Latin American cultures are known for their strong family ties, their *qué será será* attitude about life (whatever happens, happens), and their ability to celebrate in a grand way. Younger generations are becoming more proactive and independent than older generations were. Across the cluster as a whole, there are growing attempts to leave Latin traditions behind. There's a strong sense of hope and optimism about the future.

LATIN EUROPE: Found in places like France, French-speaking Canada, Italy, Portugal, Spain

Latin Europe is sometimes referred to as the cradle of Europe. This is where the European miracle began, on the shores of the Mediterranean Sea. One of the most distinctive characteristics of Latin Europe is its paternalistic orientation. Those with greater privilege, power, influence, and money should use their resources to take care of those who have not been given as much. Although fewer contemporary Latin Europeans might think of themselves as religiously devout, the values and ethos of the Roman Catholic Church still carry a lot of weight in how many Latin Europeans think and behave.

NORDIC EUROPE: Found in places like Denmark, Finland, Iceland, Norway, Sweden

Nordic means "north," and the Nordic cluster is the ancient land and people of the Norsemen, or Vikings. *Jante Law*, made popular by Danish author Aksel Sandemose, is one of the most important ideas to understand about the Nordic cluster. The overarching rule of Jante Law is: "Don't think you're anything special." Modesty, equality, humility, and skepticism are all expressions of Jante Law. In addition, Nordic cultures place the utmost value on work/life balance and believe that a society is better when people maintain a quality of life that is not solely about work and productivity.

SOUTHERN ASIA: Found in places like India, Indonesia, Malaysia, Philippines, Thailand

The cultures across Southern Asia abound with diversity; in fact, the colorful diversity of Southern Asia is its most unifying theme. This cluster has a long history of the peaceful and interactive coexistence of very diverse groups. Muslims, Sikhs, Buddhists, Hindus, Christians, and many others live and work together. The cluster is traditionally very hierarchical and service, honor, and respect are considered some of the most important ways to treat guests, elderly, and high-status people. A respect for the abundant differences in diet, languages, customs, and religion is expected of others who interact with people from this cluster.

SUB-SAHARAN AFRICA: Found in places like Ghana, Kenya, Namibia, Nigeria, Zambia, Zimbabwe

Most cultures across Africa have long, storied histories, and Sub-Saharan Africa is widely believed to be the place where human civilization began. When many people think of Africa, they think primarily of poverty, corruption, and disease; but Africa is rising. One BBC poll found that 90 percent of Africans surveyed are proud to be African and consider themselves to be successful and thriving. Many companies from around the globe are prioritizing a presence in Africa. A crucial value to understand about the Sub-Saharan Africa cluster is *ubuntu*—a ruthless commitment to interdependence and connectivity.

See my book *Expand Your Borders* for a fuller description of each of these ten cultural clusters.

RESOURCES FROM THE CULTURAL
INTELLIGENCE CENTER

The Cultural Intelligence Center (CQC) is dedicated to helping people and organizations reach their global potential through improved intercultural effectiveness.

CQ Assessments

CQC offers a variety of customized assessments for assessing and developing cultural intelligence. Current offerings include the *CQ Multi-Rater Assessment* (360°) and *CQ Self-Assessments* specifically developed for workplace settings, study-abroad trips, short-term mission groups, faith-based work, and age-specific groups. CQC also offers the *Individual Cultural Values Inventory*.

CQ Certification Programs

CQC offers programs that certify individuals to use the suite of CQ Assessments in their organization or as consultants and trainers with other clients.

CQ Research

CQC conducts ongoing research on CQ and is interested in collaborating with other researchers in the field.

CQ Consulting and Training

CQC offers face-to-face and online training resources for assessing and improving CQ. The center also provides consulting for creating a more culturally intelligent organization.

Visit www.culturalQ.com for more information.

Preface

1. Soon Ang and Linn Van Dyne, "Conceptualization of Cultural Intelligence," in *Handbook of Cultural Intelligence: Theory, Measurement, and Applications,* ed. Soon Ang and Linn Van Dyne (Armonk, NY: M.E. Sharpe, 2008), 3.
2. Aimin Yan and Yadong Luo, *International Joint Ventures: Theory and Practice* (Armonk, NY: M.E. Sharpe, 2000), 32.
3. R. J. Sternberg and D. K. Detterman, *What Is Intelligence? Contemporary Viewpoints on Its Nature and Definition* (Norwood, NJ: Ablex, 1986).
4. S. Ang et al., "Cultural Intelligence: Its Measurement and Effects on Cultural Judgment and Decision-Making, Cultural Adaptation, and Task Performance," *Management and Organization Review* 3 (2007): 335–71.
5. A compilation of much of the CQ research conducted to date is reported in Soon Ang and Linn Van Dyne, eds., *Handbook of Cultural Intelligence: Theory, Measurement, and Applications* (Armonk, NY: M.E. Sharpe, 2008).

Chapter 1: Culture Matters: Why You Need Cultural Intelligence

1. Soon Ang and Linn Van Dyne, "Conceptualization of Cultural Intelligence," in *Handbook of Cultural Intelligence: Theory, Measurement, and Applications,* ed. Soon Ang and Linn Van Dyne (Armonk, NY: M.E. Sharpe, 2008), 3.
2. Thomas Friedman, *The World Is Flat: A Brief History of the Twenty-First Century* (New York: Farrar, Straus & Giroux, 2005).
3. Economist Intelligence Unit, "CEO Briefing: Corporate Priorities for 2006 and Beyond," 2006, http://a330.g.akamai.net/7/330/25828/20060213195601/graphics.eiu.com/files/ad_pdfs/ceo_Briefing_UKTI_wp.pdf, 3.
4. Ibid., 5.
5. Ibid., 9.
6. Economist Intelligence Unit, "Competing Across Borders: How Cultural and Communication Barriers Affect Business," April 2012, http://www.economistinsights.com/countries-trade-investment/analysis/competing-across-borders.
7. Gary Ferraro, *The Cultural Dimension of International Business* (Upper Saddle River, NJ: Prentice-Hall, 2006), 2–3.
8. Economist Intelligence Unit, "CEO Briefing," 9.
9. Economist Intelligence Unit, "Competing Across Borders."
10. Economist Intelligence Unit, "CEO Briefing," 9.
11. Economist Intelligence Unit, "Competing Across Borders."

12. Douglas A. Ready, Linder A. Hill, and Jay A. Conger, "Winning the Race for Talent in Emerging Markets," *Harvard Business Review* (November 2008): 63–70.

13. Jessica R. Mesmer-Magnus and Chockalingham Viswesvaran, "Expatriate Management: A Review and Directions for Research in Expatriate Selection, Training, and Repatriation," in *Handbook of Research in International Human Resource Management*, ed. Michael Harris (Boca Raton, FL: CRC Press, 2007), 184; Linda J. Stroh et al., *International Assignments: An Integration of Strategy, Research, and Practice* (Boca Raton, FL: CRC Press, 2004).

14. Margaret Shaffer and Gloria Miller, "Cultural Intelligence: A Key Success Factor for Expatriates," in *Handbook of Cultural Intelligence: Theory, Measurement, and Applications*, ed. Soon Ang and Linn Van Dyne (Armonk, NY: M.E. Sharpe, 2008), 107, 120.

15. Bruce Brown in Jeff Dyer and Hal Gregersen, "How Procter & Gamble Keeps Its Innovation Edge," *Forbes*, April 12, 2012, http://www.forbes.com/sites/innovatorsdna/2012/04/12/how-procter-gamble-keeps-its-innovation-edge/.

16. Chris Gibbons, "The Top Team," *Acumen*, October 2013, 35.

17. Friedman, *The World Is Flat*.

18. Robert A. Kenney, Jim Blascovich, and Phillip R. Shaver, "Implicit Leadership Theories: Prototypes for New Leaders," *Basic and Applied Social Psychology* 15, no. 4 (1994): 409–37.

Chapter 2: What Is Cultural Intelligence?

1. Cheryl Tay, Mina Westman, and Audrey Chia, "Antecedents and Consequences of Cultural Intelligence Among Short-Term Business Travelers," in *Handbook of Cultural Intelligence: Theory, Measurement, and Applications*, ed. Soon Ang and Linn Van Dyne (Armonk, NY: M.E. Sharpe, 2008), 130.

2. Linn Van Dyne et al., "Sub-dimensions of the Four Factor Model of Cultural Intelligence: Expanding the Conceptualization and Measurement of Cultural Intelligence," *Social and Personality Psychology Compass* 6 (2012): 295–313.

3. Ibid.

4. Ibid.

5. Ibid.

6. Ibid.

7. S. Ang et al., "Cultural Intelligence: Its Measurement and Effects on Cultural Judgment and Decision Making, Cultural Adaptation, and Task Performance," *Management and Organization Review* 3 (2007): 335–71.

8. Van Dyne, Ang, and Koh found convergent validity between self-reported and observer-reported cultural intelligence. See Linn Van Dyne, Soon Ang, and Christine Koh, "Development and Validation of the CQS," in *Handbook*

of Cultural Intelligence: Theory, Measurement, and Applications, ed. Soon Ang and Linn Van Dyne (Armonk, NY: M.E. Sharpe, 2008), 16–38.

9. David Matsumoto and Hyisung C. Hwang, "Assessing Cross-Cultural Competence: A Review of Available Tests," *Journal of Cross-Cultural Psychology* 44 (2013): 855.

10. Ibid., 867.

11. R. J. Sternberg and D. K. Detterman, eds., *What Is Intelligence? Contemporary Viewpoints on Its Nature and Definition* (Norwood, NJ: Ablex, 1986).

12. J. D. Mayer and P. Salovey, "What Is Emotional Intelligence?" in *Emotional Development and Emotional Intelligence: Educational Applications*, ed. P. Salovey and D. Sluter (New York: Basic Books, 1997), 3–31.

13. M. Janssens and T. Cappellen, "Contextualizing Cultural Intelligence: The Case of Global Managers," in *Handbook of Cultural Intelligence: Theory, Measurement, and Applications*, ed. Soon Ang and Linn Van Dyne (Armonk, NY: M.E. Sharpe, 2008), 369.

14. Soon Ang, Linn Van Dyne, and Christine Koh, "Personality Correlates of the Four-Factor Model of Cultural Intelligence," *Group & Organizational Management* 31 (2006): 100–123.

15. Van Dyne et al., "Sub-dimensions of the Four Factor Model of Cultural Intelligence."

16. Linda Fenty, personal conversation, May 1, 2008.

Chapter 3: CQ Drive: Discover the Potential

1. Linn Van Dyne et al., "Sub-dimensions of the Four Factor Model of Cultural Intelligence: Expanding the Conceptualization and Measurement of Cultural Intelligence," *Social and Personality Psychology Compass* 6 (2012): 295–313.

2. A. Bandura, *Self-efficacy: The Exercise of Control* (New York: W. H. Freeman, 1997), 15.

3. Klaus Templer, C. Tay, and N. A. Chandrasekar, "Motivational Cultural Intelligence, Realistic Job Preview, Realistic Living Conditions Preview, and Cross-Cultural Adjustment," *Group & Organization Management* 31, no. 1 (2006): 167–68.

4. P. Christopher Earley, Soon Ang, and Joo-Seng Tan, *CQ: Developing Cultural Intelligence at Work* (Stanford, CA: Stanford Business Books, 2006), 69.

5. Cheryl Tay, Mina Westman, and Audrey Chia, "Antecedents and Consequences of Cultural Intelligence Among Short-Term Business Travelers," in *Handbook of Cultural Intelligence: Theory, Measurement, and Applications*, ed. Soon Ang and Linn Van Dyne (Armonk, NY: M.E. Sharpe, 2008), 130.

6. Earley, Ang, and Tan, *CQ*, 67–68.

7. Craig Storti, *The Art of Crossing Cultures* (Yarmouth, ME: Intercultural Press, 1990), 44.

8. W. Maddux et al., "Expanding Opportunities by Opening Your Mind: Multicultural Engagement Predicts Job Market Success Through Longitudinal Increases in Integrative Complexity," *Social Psychological and Personality Science*, December 11, 2013.
9. John Elkington, "Towards the Sustainable Corporation: Win-Win-Win Business Strategies for Sustainable Development," *California Management Review* 36, no. 2 (1994): 90–100.
10. Thich Nhat Hanh, *The Art of Power* (New York: Harper One, 2007), 68.
11. Paulo Freire, *Pedagogy of the Oppressed* (New York: Continuum, 1997).
12. Fareed Zakaria, *The Post-American World* (New York: Norton, 2008), 224.
13. Ibid., 226.
14. Henry Cloud, *Integrity: The Courage to Meet the Demands of Reality* (New York: HarperCollins, 2006), 242.
15. L. M. Shannon and T. M. Begley, "Antecedents of the Four-Factor Model of Cultural Intelligence," in *Handbook of Cultural Intelligence: Theory, Measurement, and Applications*, ed. Soon Ang and Linn Van Dyne (Armonk, NY: M.E. Sharpe, 2008), 41–54; Ibraiz Tarique and Riki Takeuchi, "Developing Cultural Intelligence: The Role of International Nonwork Experiences," in *Handbook of Cultural Intelligence: Theory, Measurement, and Applications*, ed. Soon Ang and Linn Van Dyne (Armonk, NY: M.E. Sharpe, 2008), 56.

Chapter 4: CQ Knowledge (Part 1): Know What Differences Matter

1. Allan Hall, Tom Bawden, and Sarah Butler, "Wal-Mart Pulls Out of Germany at a Cost of $1bn," *The Times*, July 29, 2006.
2. Edgar Schein, *Organizational Culture and Leadership* (San Francisco: Jossey-Bass, 2004), 11.
3. Linn Van Dyne et al., "Sub-dimensions of the Four Factor Model of Cultural Intelligence: Expanding the Conceptualization and Measurement of Cultural Intelligence," *Social and Personality Psychology Compass* 6 (2012): 295–313.
4. C. Kluckhohn and W. H. Kelly, "The Concept of Culture," in *The Science of Man in the World Crisis*, ed. R. Linton (New York: Columbia University Press, 1945), 78–105.
5. Claudia Strauss and Naomi Quinn, *A Cognitive Theory of Cultural Meaning* (Cambridge: Cambridge University Press, 1997), 253.
6. William Rugh, "If Saddam Had Been a Fulbrighter," *Christian Science Monitor*, November 2, 1995.
7. William Kiehl, *America's Dialogue with the World* (Washington, DC: Public Diplomacy Council, 2006), 42.
8. *Baywatch*. http://en.wikipedia.org/wiki/Baywatch. Accessed August 24, 2007.

9. Gary Ferraro, *The Cultural Dimension of International Business* (Upper Saddle River, NJ: Prentice-Hall, 2006), 12.

10. S. T. Shen, M. Wooley, and S. Prior, "Towards Culture-Centered Design," *Interacting with Computers* 18 (2006): 820–52.

11. R. J. House et al., *Culture, Leadership, and Organizations: The GLOBE Study of 62 Societies* (Thousand Oaks, CA: Sage, 2004).

12. Ferraro, *The Cultural Dimension of International Business*, 48.

13. Ibid., 49.

14. R. Parkin, *Kinship: An Introduction to Basic Concepts* (Malden, MA: Blackwell, 1997), 49.

15. Kwok Leung and Soon Ang, "Culture, Organizations, and Institutions," in *Cambridge Handbook of Culture, Organizations, and Work*, ed. R. S. Bhagat and R. M. Steers (Cambridge: Cambridge University Press, 2008), 26.

16. M. Weber, *The Protestant Ethic and the Spirit of Capitalism* (New York: Charles Scribner's Sons, 1958).

17. Leung and Ang, "Culture, Organizations, and Institutions," 29.

18. A. Ong, *Spirits of Resistance and Capitalist Discipline: Factory Women in Malaysia* (Albany: State University of New York Press, 1987), 101.

19. Paul Hiebert, *Anthropological Reflections on Missiological Issues* (Grand Rapids, MI: Baker Academic, 1994), 114.

20. Ibid., 113.

Chapter 5: CQ Knowledge (Part 2): Understand Ten Cultural Value Dimensions

1. Check out *Cultures and Organizations, Riding the Waves of Culture, From Foreign to Familiar,* and *The Silent Language* as great places to begin. The first two and others are cited throughout this chapter.

2. Geert Hofstede, Gert Jan Hofstede, and Michael Minkov, *Cultures and Organizations: Software of the Mind* (New York: McGraw-Hill, 2010), 89–134.

3. My experience closely mirrors a simulation referenced in Craig Storti, *Cross-Cultural Dialogues* (Yarmouth, ME: Intercultural Press, 1994), 64. Storti's analysis helped my own thinking about the role of hierarchy in this encounter.

4. L. Robert Kohls and John Knight, *Developing Intercultural Awareness: A Cross-Cultural Training Handbook* (Yarmouth, ME: Intercultural Press, 1994), 45.

5. Hofstede, Hofstede, and Minkov, *Cultures and Organizations*, 53–87.

6. David Livermore, "How Facebook Develops Its Global Leaders: Conversation with Bill McLawhon," *People and Strategy* 36 (2013): 24–25.

7. Hofstede, Hofstede, and Minkov, *Cultures and Organizations*, 187–233.

8. Soon Ang, personal conversation, October 26, 2005; M. J. Gelfand, L. Nishii, and J. Raver, "On the Nature and Importance of Cultural Tightness-Looseness," *Journal of Applied Psychology* 91 (2006): 1225–44.

9. Hofstede, Hofstede, and Minkov, *Cultures and Organizations*, 135–84; note that Hofstede et al. refer to this dimension as feminine versus masculine but many have moved away from using these terms lest they perpetuate gender stereotypes.

10. Ibid., 235–74.

11. Ibid.

12. Edward Hall, *The Hidden Dimension* (New York: Anchor Books, 1969), 77–95.

13. Patty Lane, *A Beginner's Guide to Crossing Cultures* (Downers Grove, IL: InterVarsity Press, 2002), 61–71.

14. Fons Trompenaars and Charles Hampden-Turner, *Riding the Waves of Culture: Understanding Diversity in Global Business* (New York: McGraw-Hill, 1997), 125–56.

15. Andres Tapia, *The Inclusion Paradox: The Obama Era and the Transformation of Global Diversity* (Chicago: Andres Tapia, 2009), 112–113.

16. Trompenaars and Hampden-Turner, *Riding the Waves of Culture*, 78–103.

17. Hall, *The Hidden Dimension*, 122–45.

18. As noted in the citations throughout this chapter, a number of scholars have contributed to the research on cultural value dimensions, including Geert Hofstede, Fons Trompenaars, and Edward Hall. My colleagues and I have benefited a great deal from this work and have also built on it by doing our own research and analysis of the ten cultural dimensions included. For more information on how to assess your individual orientation on these ten dimensions, visit www.culturalQ.com.

19. J. S. Osland and A. Bird, "Beyond Sophisticated Stereotyping: Cultural Sense Making in Context," *Academy of Management Executive* 14, no. 1 (2000): 65–80.

Chapter 6: CQ Strategy: Don't Trust Your Gut

1. Linn Van Dyne et al., "Sub-dimensions of the Four Factor Model of Cultural Intelligence: Expanding the Conceptualization and Measurement of Cultural Intelligence," *Social and Personality Psychology Compass* 6 (2012): 295–313.

2. P. Christopher Earley and Soon Ang, *Cultural Intelligence: Individual Interactions Across Cultures* (Stanford: Stanford Business Books, 2003), 115.

3. Tom Rath, *StrengthsFinder 2.0: A New and Upgraded Edition of the Online Test from Gallup's Now, Discover Your Strengths* (Washington, DC: Gallup Press, 2007).

4. P. Christopher Earley, Soon Ang, and Joo-Seng Tan, *CQ: Developing Cultural Intelligence at Work* (Stanford, CA: Stanford University Press, 2006), 11.

5. Soon Ang and Linn Van Dyne, "Conceptualization of Cultural Intelligence," in *Handbook of Cultural Intelligence: Theory, Measurement, and Applications,* ed. Soon Ang and Linn Van Dyne (Armonk, NY: M.E. Sharpe, 2008), 5.

6. R. Brislin, R. Worthley, and B. Macnab, "Cultural Intelligence: Understanding Behaviors That Serve People's Goals," *Group and Organization Management* 31, no. 1 (February 2006): 49.

7. Six Sigma Financial Services, "Determine the Root Cause: 5 Whys," http://finance.isixsigma.com/library/content/c020610a.asp.

8. Kok Yee Ng, Linn Van Dyne, and Soon Ang, "From Experience to Experiential Learning: Cultural Intelligence as a Learning Capability for Global Leader Development," *Academy of Management Learning & Education* 8 (2009): 29.

Chapter 7: CQ Action: Be Yourself, Sort Of

1. Edward Stewart and Milton Bennett, *American Cultural Patterns: A Cross-Cultural Perspective* (Boston: Intercultural Press, 1991), 15.

2. Linn Van Dyne et al., "Sub-dimensions of the Four Factor Model of Cultural Intelligence: Expanding the Conceptualization and Measurement of Cultural Intelligence," *Social and Personality Psychology Compass* 6 (2012): 295–313.

3. University of Phoenix is a for-profit institution that specializes in adult education with more than 100,000 students across numerous campuses.

4. Van Dyne et al., "Sub-dimensions of the Four Factor Model of Cultural Intelligence."

5. Helen Spencer-Oatey, "Rapport Management," in *Culturally Speaking,* ed. Helen Spencer-Oatey (London: Continuum Press, 2000), 236–37.

6. Adapted from Helen Spencer-Oatey's example of asking someone to wash the dishes in Spencer-Oatey, "Rapport Management," 22.

7. Originally reported in my book *Cultural Intelligence: Improving Your CQ to Engage Our Multicultural World* (Grand Rapids, MI: Baker Books, 2008), 115.

8. Peter Hays Gries and Kaiping Peng, "Culture Clash? Apologies East and West," *Journal of Contemporary China* 11 (2002): 173–78.

9. Gary Ferraro, *The Cultural Dimension of International Business* (Upper Saddle River, NJ: Prentice-Hall, 2006), 90–92.

10. David Thomas and Kerr Inkson, *Cultural Intelligence: People Skills for Global Business* (San Francisco: Berrett-Koehler, 2004), 113.

11. Ibid., 116.

12. Research findings on CQ and negotiation presented in Lynn Imai and Michele J. Gelfand, "The Culturally Intelligent Negotiator: The Impact of Cultural Intelligence (CQ) on Negotiation Sequences and Outcomes," *Organizational Behavior and Human Decision Processes* 112 (2010): 83–98; L. Imai and M. J. Gelfand, "Culturally Intelligent Negotiators: The Impact

of CQ on Intercultural Negotiation Effectiveness," *Academy of Management Best Paper Proceedings* (2007).

13. Jeswald W. Salacuse, *The Global Negotiator: Making, Managing, and Mending Deals Around the World in the Twenty-First Century* (New York: Palgrave Macmillan, 2003).

14. Ibid., 172.

15. H. Giles and P. Smith, "Accommodation Theory: Optimal Levels of Convergence," in *Language and Social Psychology*, ed. H. Giles and R. N. St. Clair (Baltimore: University Park Press, 1979), 45–63.

16. Michele J. Gelfand et al., "Differences Between Tight and Loose Cultures: A 33-Nation Study," *Science* 27 (May 2011): 1100–1104.

Chapter 8: The ROI for Culturally Intelligent Leaders

1. S. Ang, L. Van Dyne, and T. Rockstuhl, "Cultural Intelligence: Origins, Conceptualization, Evolution, and Methodological Diversity," in *Advances in Culture and Psychology: Volume 5*, ed. M. Gelfand, C. Chiu, and Y. Y. Hong (New York: Oxford University Press, 2014, in press).

2. Soon Ang, Linn Van Dyne, and Christine Koh, "Personality Correlates of the Four-Factor Model of Cultural Intelligence," *Group & Organizational Management* 31 (2006): 100–123.

3. Efrat Shokef and Miriam Erea, "Cultural Intelligence and Global Identity in Multicultural Teams," in *Handbook of Cultural Intelligence: Theory, Measurement, and Applications*, ed. Soon Ang and Linn Van Dyne (Armonk, NY: M.E. Sharpe, 2008), 180.

4. Cheryl Tay, Mina Westman, and Audrey Chia, "Antecedents and Consequences of Cultural Intelligence Among Short-Term Business Travelers," in *Handbook of Cultural Intelligence: Theory, Measurement, and Applications*, ed. Soon Ang and Linn Van Dyne (Armonk, NY: M.E. Sharpe, 2008), 126–44; S. Ang et al., "Cultural Intelligence: Its Measurement and Effects on Cultural Judgment and Decision Making, Cultural Adaptation, and Task Performance," *Management and Organization Review* 3 (2007): 335–71; L. M. Shannon and T. M. Begley, "Antecedents of the Four-Factor Model of Cultural Intelligence," in *Handbook of Cultural Intelligence: Theory, Measurement, and Applications*, ed. Soon Ang and Linn Van Dyne (Armonk, NY: M.E. Sharpe, 2008), 41–55.

5. Tay, Westman, and Chia, "Antecedents and Consequences," 126–44.

6. Shokef and Erez, "Cultural Intelligence and Global Identity," 177–91.

7. Ang, Van Dyne, and Rockstuhl, "Cultural Intelligence: Origins, Conceptualization, Evolution, and Methodological Diversity."

8. M. Abdul Malek and P. Budhwar, "Cultural Intelligence as a Predictor of Expatriate Adjustment and Performance in Malaysia," *Journal of World Business* 48 (2013): 222–31; G. Chen et al., "When Does Intercultural

Motivation Enhance Expatriate Effectiveness? A Multilevel Investigation of the Moderating Roles of Subsidiary Support and Cultural Distance," *Academy of Management Journal* 53 (2010): 1110–30; L. Y. Lee and B. M. Sukoco, "The Effects of Cultural Intelligence on Expatriate Performance: The Moderating Effects of International Experience," *International Journal of Human Resource Management* 21 (2010): 963–81; Y. C. Lin, A. Chen, and Y. C. Song, "Does Your Intelligence Help to Survive in a Foreign Jungle? The Effects of Cultural Intelligence and Emotional Intelligence on Cross-Cultural Adjustment," *International Journal of Intercultural Relations* 36 (2012): 541–52; H. K. Moon, B. K. Choi, and J. S. Jung, "Previous International Experience, Intercultural Training, and Expatriates' Intercultural Adjustment: Effects of Cultural Intelligence and Goal Orientation," *Human Resource Development Quarterly* 23 (2012): 285–330; S. Sri Ramalu et al., "Cultural Intelligence and Expatriate Performance in Global Assignment: The Mediating Role of Adjustment," *International Journal of Business and Society* 13 (2012): 19–32; C. Ward et al., "The Convergent, Discriminant, and Incremental Validity of Scores on a Self-Report Measure of Cultural Intelligence," *Educational and Psychological Measurement* 69 (2009): 85–105; P. C. Wu and S. H. Ang, "The Impact of Expatriate Supporting Practices and Cultural Intelligence on Intercultural Adjustment and Performance of Expatriates in Singapore," *International Journal of Human Resource Management* 22 (2012): 2683–2702.

9. T. Oolders, O. S. Chernyshenko, and S. Shark, "Cultural Intelligence as a Mediator of Relationships Between Openness to Experience and Adaptive Performance," in *Handbook of Cultural Intelligence: Theory, Measurement, and Applications*, ed. S. Ang and L. Van Dyne (Armonk, NY: M.E. Sharpe, 2008), 145–58; Ang et al., "Cultural Intelligence: Its Measurement and Effects."

10. Linn Van Dyne, Soon Ang, and Christine Koh, "Development and Validation of the CQS," in *Handbook of Cultural Intelligence: Theory, Measurement, and Applications*, ed. Soon Ang and Linn Van Dyne (Armonk, NY: M.E. Sharpe, 2008), 16–38.

11. Tay, Westman, and Chia, "Antecedents and Consequences of Cultural Intelligence," 126ff.

12. Economist Intelligence Unit, "CEO Briefing: Corporate Priorities for 2006 and Beyond," 2006, http://a330.g.akamai.net/7/330/25828/20060213195601/graphics.eiu.com/files/ad_pdfs/ceo_Briefing_UKTI_wp.pdf, 14.

13. P. Christopher Earley, Soon Ang, and Joo-Seng Tan, *CQ: Developing Cultural Intelligence at Work* (Stanford, CA: Stanford Business Books, 2006), 10.

14. Ang et al., "Cultural Intelligence: Its Measurement and Effects."

15. Lynn Imai and Michele J. Gelfand, "The Culturally Intelligent Negotiator: The Impact of Cultural Intelligence (CQ) on Negotiation Sequences and

Outcomes," *Organizational Behavior and Human Decision Processes* 112 (2010): 83–98.

16. Ibid.; Roy Y. J. Chua, Michael W. Morris, and Shira Mor, "Collaborating Across Cultures: Cultural Metacognition and Affect-Based Trust in Creative Collaboration," *Organizational Behavior and Human Decision Processes* 118 (2012): 116–31.

17. Eva Cheng, personal conversation, Hong Kong, March 10, 2014.

18. Ibid.

19. K. S. Groves and A. E. Feyerherm, "Leader Cultural Intelligence in Context: Testing the Moderating Effects of Team Cultural Diversity on Leader and Team Performance," *Group & Organization Management* 36 (2011): 535–66; Ang et al., "Cultural Intelligence: Its Measurement and Effects."

20. Ang, Van Dyne, and Rockstuhl, "Cultural Intelligence: Origins, Conceptualization, Evolution, and Methodological Diversity."

21. David Livermore, "How Facebook Develops Its Global Leaders: Conversation with Bill McLawhon," *People and Strategy* 36 (2013): 24–25.

22. Ang et al., "Cultural Intelligence: Its Measurement and Effects."

23. T. Rockstuhl et al., *International Military Officer Potential: Effects of Cultural Capital on Cultural Intelligence* (Working Paper, Nanyang Business School, Singapore, 2014); T. Rockstuhl et al., *Beyond International Experience: Effects of Cultural Capital on Cultural Intelligence.* Paper presented at the Academy of Management Annual Meeting, Orlando, FL, August 2013.

24. Chua, Morris, and Mor, "Collaborating Across Cultures"; T. Rockstuhl and K. Y. Ng, "The Effects of Cultural Intelligence on Interpersonal Trust in Multicultural Teams," in *Handbook of Cultural Intelligence: Theory, Measurement, and Applications,* ed. S. Ang and L. Van Dyne (Armonk, NY: M.E. Sharpe, 2008), 206–220.

25. Daniel Pink, *To Sell Is Human: The Surprising Truth About Moving Others* (New York: Riverhead Books, 2012), 158.

26. Economist Intelligence Unit, "CEO Briefing," 14.

27. X. P. Chen, D. Liu, and R. Portnoy, "A Multilevel Investigation of Motivational Cultural Intelligence, Organizational Diversity Climate, and Cultural Sales: Evidence from U.S. Real Estate Firms," *Journal of Applied Psychology* 97 (2012): 93–106.

28. R. Nouri et al., "Taking the Bite Out of Culture: The Impact of Task Structure and Task Type on Overcoming Impediments to Cross-Cultural Team Performance," *Journal of Organizational Behavior* (in press); Chua, Morris, and Mor, "Collaborating Across Cultures."

29. Visit www.culturalQ.com for more information on the *CQ Multi-Rater Assessment.*

30. Earley, Ang, and Tan, *CQ,* 10.

31. S. K. Crotty and J. M. Brett, "Fusing Creativity: Cultural Metacognition and Teamwork in Multicultural Teams," *Negotiation and Conflict Management*

Research 5 (2012): 210–34; L. M. Moynihan, R. S. Peterson, and P. C. Earley, "Cultural Intelligence and the Multinational Team Experience: Does the Experience of Working in a Multinational Team Improve Cultural Intelligence?" *Research on Managing Groups and Teams* 9 (2006): 299–323; W. L. Adair, I. Hideg, and J. R. Spence, "The Culturally Intelligent Team: The Impact of Team Cultural Intelligence and Cultural Heterogeneity on Team Shared Values," *Journal of Cross-Cultural Psychology* 44 (2013): 941–62.

32. Economist Intelligence Unit, "Competing Across Borders: How Cultural and Communication Barriers Affect Business," April 2012, http://www. economistinsights.com/countries-trade-investment/analysis/competing-across-borders.

33. Rhonda Colvin, "The Cost of Expanding Overseas," *Wall Street Journal,* February 27, 2014, B6.

34. Abraham Sorock, "The Expat's Competitive Edge: Technical Skills, Cross-Cultural Knowledge, and Language Abilities Can Help Expats in China Find Positions in a Competitive Market," October 21, 2013, http://100kstrong. org/2013/11/01/china-business-review-the-expats-competitive-edge/.

35. Brian Carroll, "China Daily USA, Apco Worldwide Examine Experiences Facing Chinese Enterprises Doing Business in United States: Joint Study Identifies Key Factors for Success," February 25, 2013, http://www. apcoworldwide.com/content/news/press_releases2013/china_daily_ research0225.aspx.

36. K. Kim, B. L. Kirkman, and G. Chen, "Cultural Intelligence and International Assignment Effectiveness," in *Handbook of Cultural Intelligence: Theory, Measurement, and Applications*, ed. S. Ang and L. Van Dyne (Armonk, NY: M.E. Sharpe, 2008), 71–90; Ramalu et al., "Cultural Intelligence and Expatriate Performance in Global Assignment"; S. Sri Ramalu, F. M. Shamsudin, and C. Subramaniam, "The Mediating Effect of Cultural Intelligence on the Relationship Between Openness Personality and Job Performance Among Expatriates on International Assignments," *International Business Management* 6 (2012): 601–10.

37. Earley, Ang, and Tan, *CQ,* 10.

38. Soon Ang and Andrew C. Inkpen, "Cultural Intelligence and Offshore Outsourcing Success: A Framework of Firm-Level Intercultural Capability," *Decision Sciences* 39, no. 3 (2008): 346.

39. Ang, Van Dyne, and Rockstuhl, "Cultural Intelligence: Origins, Conceptualization, Evolution, and Methodological Diversity."

Chapter 9: Developing a Culturally Intelligent Team

1. Soon Ang and Andrew C. Inkpen, "Cultural Intelligence and Offshore Outsourcing Success: A Framework of Firm-Level Intercultural Capability," *Decision Sciences* 39, no. 3 (2008): 343–44; M. A. Carpenter, W. G. Sanders,

and H. B. Gregersen, "Bundling Human Capital with Organizational Context: The Impact of International Assignment Experience on Multinational Firm Performance and CEO Pay," *Academy Management Journal* 44, no. 3 (2001): 493–511.

2. Jeffrey Liker, *The Toyota Way: 14 Management Principles from the World's Greatest Manufacturer* (New York: McGraw-Hill, 2004), 228–30.

3. Ang and Inkpen, "Cultural Intelligence and Offshore Outsourcing Success," 346.

4. Maddy Janssens and Tineke Cappellen, "Contextualizing Cultural Intelligence: The Case of Global Managers," in *Handbook of Cultural Intelligence: Theory, Measurement, and Applications*, ed. Soon Ang and Linn Van Dyne (Armonk, NY: M.E. Sharpe, 2008), 369.

5. P. Christopher Earley, Soon Ang, and Joo-Seng Tan, *CQ: Developing Cultural Intelligence at Work* (Stanford, CA: Stanford Business Books, 2006), 29.

6. Michael Goh, Julie M. Koch, and Sandra Sanger, "Cultural Intelligence in Counseling Psychology," in *Handbook of Cultural Intelligence: Theory, Measurement, and Applications*, ed. Soon Ang and Linn Van Dyne (Armonk, NY: M.E. Sharpe, 2008), 264.

7. Margaret Shaffer and Gloria Miller, "Cultural Intelligence: A Key Success Factor for Expatriates," in *Handbook of Cultural Intelligence: Theory, Measurement, and Applications*, ed. Soon Ang and Linn Van Dyne (Armonk, NY: M.E. Sharpe, 2008), 107ff.

8. Cheryl Tay, Mina Westman, and Audrey Chia, "Antecedents and Consequences of Cultural Intelligence Among Short-Term Business Travelers," in *Handbook of Cultural Intelligence: Theory, Measurement, and Applications*, ed. Soon Ang and Linn Van Dyne (Armonk, NY: M.E. Sharpe, 2008), 130.

Epilogue

1. Edgar Schein, *Organizational Culture and Leadership* (San Francisco: Jossey-Bass, 2004), 23.

Appendix 1: Ten Cultural Clusters

1. Simcha Ronen and Oded Shenkar, "Clustering Countries on Attitudinal Dimensions: A Review and Synthesis," *Academy of Management Review* 10, no. 3 (July 1985): 435-442.

ABOUT THE AUTHOR

David Livermore, PhD (Michigan State University), has written several books about cultural intelligence and global leadership. He is president of the Cultural Intelligence Center in East Lansing, Michigan (www.culturalQ.com), and a visiting scholar at Nanyang Technological University in Singapore. He has done consulting and training with leaders in more than a hundred countries. David and his family live in Grand Rapids, Michigan. Visit his work at www.davidlivermore.com and www.culturalQ.com.